Welcome to the magical world of sourdough baking!

If you're opening this guide, you're probably looking to embark on a delightful journey that not only fills your kitchen with the warm, comforting aroma of freshly baked bread but also introduces you to a craft as old as civilization itself.

Fear not, dear beginner, for this guide is crafted with you in mind, designed to demystify the art of sourdough bread making in the most engaging and comprehensive manner.

Before we dive into the detailed instructions, it's essential to familiarize yourself with a few key concepts and terms you'll encounter along this journey. Understanding these basics will not only make the process more enjoyable but also demystify some of the magic behind sourdough bread.

What is Sourdough?

Sourdough is a method of bread baking that uses a fermented mixture of flour and water, known as a "starter," to leaven the bread instead of commercial yeast. This technique has been used for thousands of years and is cherished for its depth of flavor, tangy sour notes, and hearty texture.

The Sourdough Starter

The heart of any sourdough bread is its starter. Think of it as a living community of wild yeast and beneficial bacteria that are naturally present in flour. These microorganisms ferment the dough, causing it to rise and develop its characteristic flavor and texture. Creating and maintaining a sourdough starter involves mixing flour and water and allowing it to ferment over several days, feeding it regularly to keep it active and healthy.

Autolyse: The First Step in Dough Preparation

Autolyse (pronounced "auto-lease") is a simple yet crucial step in the sourdough bread-making process. It involves mixing just the flour and water from your recipe and letting it rest for a period (usually 30 minutes to an hour) before adding the starter and salt. This resting period hydrates the flour, starts gluten development (gluten gives bread its structure and chewiness), and ultimately makes the dough easier to shape and more flavorful. Autolyse is a secret weapon in bread making that enhances both the texture and taste of your sourdough.

Fermentation: Bulk Fermentation and Proofing

Fermentation is the magical process that makes sourdough bread possible. It's divided into two main stages:

Bulk Fermentation: This is the first rise of the dough after mixing all the ingredients, including the sourdough starter. During this stage, the dough will increase in volume and develop its structure and flavor. It's called "bulk" because the dough is still in one large piece.

Proofing: After the dough is shaped into loaves, it goes through another rise, known as proofing. This final rise helps the dough achieve its final size and shape before baking.

Shaping and Scoring: Shaping the dough into loaves is an art form that affects the bread's final appearance and texture. Proper shaping creates tension on the surface of the dough, which helps it rise upward instead of spreading outwards. Scoring, or making shallow cuts on the dough's surface before baking, allows the bread to expand in a controlled manner, creating those beautiful patterns you see on artisan loaves.

With these concepts in mind, you're now better prepared to start your sourdough bread-making journey.

WHAT YOU'LL NEED

Ingredients:

Flour: For starters, all-purpose or bread flour works great.

Water: Use filtered water if possible, as chlorine in tap water can inhibit the growth of your starter.

Salt: Enhances flavor. Fine sea salt is preferred.

Sourdough Starter: This is the heart of your bread, a fermented mix of flour and water teeming with wild yeast and bacteria.

Equipment:

Mixing Bowls: For mixing your dough.

Kitchen Scale: Precision is key in baking, so a scale is preferred over measuring cups.

Dough Scraper: To handle and cut your dough.

Proofing Basket (Banneton): Gives your dough shape and supports it during the final rise.

Dutch Oven: For baking. It traps steam and mimics a professional bread oven.

Linen Cloth: To line your basket or to cover the dough as it rises.

Sharp Knife: For scoring your bread before baking.

Embarking on your sourdough journey is exciting, and this detailed guide aims to provide you with a clear, step-by-step process, including precise measurements, timings, and tips to ensure your success.

Let's dive into the fascinating world of sourdough bread making!

1. Creating Your Sourdough Starter

Day 1:

- Mix 100g whole wheat flour with 100g water in a container.
- Cover loosely and let sit at room temperature (68-70°F or 20-22°C).

Day 2 to Day 7:

- Daily, discard half (about 100g) and add 100g all-purpose flour and 100g water.
- Mix well and let sit as on day 1.
- Ready when bubbly, smells sour, and doubles in volume.

2. Mixing Your Dough

Autolyse:

- Combine 500g all-purpose/bread flour with 350g water.
- Mix until no dry bits remain, then cover and rest for 30 mins to 1 hour at room temperature.

Add Starter and Salt:

- Add 100g active sourdough starter and 10g salt to the mixture.
- Mix until well incorporated.

3. Bulk Fermentation

- Let the dough rise at room temperature.
- Perform a fold every 30 minutes for the first 2 hours (total of 4 folds).
- After folding, let the dough rest until it increases by 50-75% in volume (4 to 12 hours depending on temperature).

4. Shaping Your Loaf

- Transfer the dough to a lightly floured surface.
- Fold the dough over itself from all sides, then shape into a ball or oval.
- Rest for 20-30 minutes, then do a final shaping to tighten the surface.

5. Proofing

- Place the dough seam-side up in a floured proofing basket or bowl.
- Cover and let proof for 1-2 hours at room temperature, or 12-14 hours in the refrigerator.

6. Baking

- Preheat the oven with a Dutch oven inside to 450°F (230°C) for 30 minutes.
- Gently invert the dough onto a piece of parchment paper and score the top.
- Place the dough in the hot Dutch oven, cover, and bake for 20 minutes.
- Uncover and bake for another 20-25 minutes until golden brown and the internal temperature reaches about 210°F (99°C).

7. Cooling

- Remove the bread from the Dutch oven.
- Let it cool on a wire rack for at least an hour before slicing.

Tips for Success:

Temperature Matters: The ambient temperature can significantly affect fermentation times. Warmer environments speed up fermentation, while cooler ones slow it down.

Hydration Adjustment: Depending on your flour and humidity, you might need to adjust the water amount slightly. If the dough is too sticky to handle, add a bit more flour during the initial mix.

Scoring: Your score doesn't just affect the bread's aesthetics; it also helps control how the bread expands in the oven. A shallow angle (about 30 degrees) and decisive slash can make a beautiful pattern.

Patience is Key: Sourdough bread making is as much about intuition and patience as it is about following steps. Each batch teaches you something new, so embrace the learning process.

Within the following pages, we are delighted to present you with a curated **collection of 100 exquisite recipes**, each meticulously designed to complement and enhance the unique flavors of your freshly baked sourdough bread.

Embark on a culinary journey that will elevate your home-baked sourdough to new heights, transforming it into an array of delightful dishes that promise to delight your senses and enrich your dining experience.

TABLE OF CONTENTS FOR RECIPES

Charred Corn & Jalapeno Egg Salad Sandwich

1 SERVING 20 MINUTES

INGREDIENTS

2 Egg

1 ear Corn on the Cob (husk removed)

1 1/2 tsps Mayonnaise

1/4 Lemon (juiced)

1/4 Jalapeno Pepper (seeds removed, finely diced)

1 tbsp Cilantro (chopped)

Sea Salt & Black Pepper (to taste)

3 1/2 ozs Sourdough Bread (sliced, toasted)

NUTRITION

AMOUNT PER SERVING

Calories	532	**Carbs**	69g
Fat	16g	**Protein**	25g

DIRECTIONS

01 Preheat the air fryer to 275°F (135°C). Place the eggs in the air fryer basket, in a single layer. Cook for 15 minutes, then immediately transfer to the ice bath for about five minutes.

02 Meanwhile, heat a large cast-iron skillet over medium heat. Cook the corn for one to two minutes per side until lightly charred on all sides. Once it is cooked, let it cool for about 10 minutes before slicing the kernels off the cob.

03 In a bowl, mix together the mayonnaise, lemon juice, jalapeño, cilantro, salt, and pepper. Chop the eggs and add to the bowl along with the corn. Stir to combine.

04 Spread the egg salad over one slice of sourdough. Close the sandwich and enjoy!

NOTES

LEFTOVERS
Refrigerate the egg salad in an airtight container for up to three days. Assemble the sandwich before serving.

SERVING SIZE
One serving is equal to one sandwich.

NO CILANTRO
Omit or use dill instead.

GLUTEN-FREE
Use gluten-free bread instead.

SOURDOUGH BREAD
One slice of sourdough bread is equal to approximately 1 3/4 oz or 50 grams.

NO AIR FRYER
Hard boil the eggs in a pot on the stove.

Balsamic Mushroom & Avocado Toast

1 SERVING 10 MINUTES

INGREDIENTS

1 tsp Extra Virgin Olive Oil

2 Cremini Mushrooms (sliced)

1 Garlic (clove, small, sliced)

Sea Salt & Black Pepper (to taste)

1 1/2 tsps Balsamic Vinegar

1/2 Avocado (small, sliced)

1 3/4 ozs Sourdough Bread (toasted)

NUTRITION

AMOUNT PER SERVING

Calories	344	**Carbs**	36g
Fat	19g	**Protein**	8g

DIRECTIONS

01 Heat a pan over medium heat. Add the oil, mushrooms, garlic, salt, and pepper. Sauté for three to five minutes, or until the mushrooms have softened and started to brown.

02 Add the balsamic vinegar to the pan and toss well to coat the mushrooms. Set aside.

03 Add the avocado to the sourdough and put the mushrooms on top. Enjoy!

NOTES

LEFTOVERS
Best enjoyed immediately. Cut the avocado when ready to serve.

SERVING SIZE
One serving is one piece of toast with toppings.

MORE FLAVOR
Add chili flakes, flaky salt, hot sauce, and/or fresh thyme.

GLUTEN-FREE
Use gluten-free bread.

SOURDOUGH BREAD
One slice of sourdough bread is equal to approximately 1 3/4 oz or 50 grams.

Mini Submarine Sandwich

2 SERVINGS 10 MINUTES

INGREDIENTS

2 tsps Yellow Mustard

3 ozs Provolone Cheese

4 ozs Sliced Ham

2 ozs Salami, Mild

1/4 head Iceberg Lettuce (chopped)

6 ozs Sourdough Baguette

NUTRITION

AMOUNT PER SERVING

Calories	569	**Carbs**	53g
Fat	23g	**Protein**	36g

DIRECTIONS

01 To assemble the sandwiches, evenly divide the mustard, cheese, ham, salami, and lettuce between the buns. Enjoy!

NOTES

LEFTOVERS
Best enjoyed fresh. Refrigerate in an airtight container for up to two days.

SERVING SIZE
One serving is one sandwich.

ADDITIONAL TOPPINGS
Cucumber, tomato, onions and/or hot peppers.

NO MUSTARD
Use mayonnaise or other spread of choice.

GLUTEN-FREE
Use gluten-free bread.

DAIRY-FREE
Use a dairy-free cheese alternative.

Chimichurri Corn Crostini

2 SERVINGS 10 MINUTES

INGREDIENTS

2 tbsps Parsley (chopped)

1 1/2 tbsps Extra Virgin Olive Oil

1 1/2 tbsps Lemon Juice

1 Garlic (clove, minced)

1/8 tsp Sea Salt

1/2 tsp Chili Flakes

1 cup Corn

2 ozs Sourdough Baguette (sliced, toasted)

NUTRITION

AMOUNT PER SERVING

Calories	247	Carbs	34g
Fat	12g	Protein	5g

DIRECTIONS

01 In a bowl, mix together the parsley, oil, lemon juice, garlic, salt, and chili flakes. Add the corn and stir well to combine.

02 Top the sliced baguettes with the corn mixture. Enjoy!

NOTES

LEFTOVERS
Refrigerate the corn mixture in an airtight container for up to three days.

SERVING SIZE
One serving is equal to approximately two to three crostinis.

ADDITIONAL TOPPINGS
Feta cheese.

GLUTEN-FREE
Use a gluten-free baguette or gluten-free crackers instead.

Shrimp Po' Boy

2 SERVINGS 20 MINUTES

INGREDIENTS

1/4 cup Mayonnaise

2 tsps Pickle Brine

2 stalks Green Onion (finely chopped)

1 tbsp Cajun Spice (divided)

8 ozs Shrimp (peeled, deveined, and tails off)

1 tbsp Avocado Oil

8 ozs Sourdough Baguette (split horizontally)

1 Tomato (medium, sliced)

4 leaves Romaine

NUTRITION

AMOUNT PER SERVING

Calories	687	Carbs	70g
Fat	30g	Protein	34g

DIRECTIONS

01 In a bowl, mix together the mayonnaise, brine, green onions, and 1/3 of the Cajun seasoning. Set aside.

02 In a mixing bowl, toss together the shrimp with the remaining Cajun seasoning until evenly coated.

03 Warm the oil in a large non-stick skillet over medium-high heat. Cook the shrimp until cooked through, about two to three minutes per side. Work in batches if needed for maximum crispiness.

04 Spread the mayonnaise evenly over each side of the baguette. Divide the tomato, romaine, and shrimp between the baguette(s). Close the sandwich and enjoy!

NOTES

LEFTOVERS
Best enjoyed immediately. Refrigerate the prepared ingredients, separate from the bread, in an airtight container for up to two days.

SERVING SIZE
One serving is equal to one sandwich.

MORE FLAVOR
Add mustard and roasted garlic to the mayonnaise. Add microgreens and cucumber slices. Add some flour to the Cajun seasoning that you toss the shrimp in for maximum crispiness.

ADDITIONAL TOPPINGS
Pickled onions or dill pickles.

GLUTEN-FREE
Use gluten-free baguette or bread.

Chickpea, Tuna & Roasted Red Pepper Sandwich

2 SERVINGS 10 MINUTES

INGREDIENTS

1 cup Chickpeas (cooked, rinsed)

1 can Tuna (drained)

1/2 stalk Celery (finely chopped)

2 tbsps Parsley (chopped)

1 tbsp Plain Greek Yogurt

1 1/2 tsps Lemon Juice

Sea Salt & Black Pepper (to taste)

4 ozs Roasted Red Peppers

4 slices Bread (toasted)

NUTRITION

AMOUNT PER SERVING

Calories	379	Carbs	50g
Fat	8g	Protein	28g

DIRECTIONS

01 In a bowl, lightly smash the chickpeas with the back of a fork. Mix in the tuna, celery, parsley, yogurt, lemon juice, salt, and pepper. Adjust the seasoning to your taste.

02 Assemble the sandwich by placing roasted red peppers on a slice of toast. Spoon the tuna mixture on top, and close the sandwich. Repeat for any remaining slices of toast.

03 Slice the sandwiches in half and enjoy!

NOTES

LEFTOVERS
Best enjoyed fresh. Refrigerate the chickpea mixture in an airtight container for up to two days.

SERVING SIZE
One serving is equal to one sandwich.

MORE FLAVOR
Add red onion and cucumber.

GLUTEN-FREE
Use gluten-free bread.

DAIRY-FREE
Use coconut yogurt instead of Greek yogurt.

CANNED TUNA
One can of tuna is equal to 165 grams or 5.8 ounces, drained.

Smoked Salmon & Goat Cheese Crostini

6 SERVINGS 5 MINUTES

INGREDIENTS

1/4 cup Goat Cheese

4 1/3 ozs Sourdough Baguette (sliced, toasted)

1 3/4 ozs Smoked Salmon

2 tbsps Fresh Dill (chopped)

NUTRITION

AMOUNT PER SERVING

Calories	80	**Carbs**	12g
Fat	2g	**Protein**	4g

DIRECTIONS

01 Spread the goat cheese evenly onto the toasted baguette slices. Top with smoked salmon and dill. Enjoy!

NOTES

LEFTOVERS
Best enjoyed immediately.

SERVING SIZE
One serving is equal to approximately two crostinis.

ADDITIONAL TOPPINGS
Top with capers.

GLUTEN-FREE
Use a gluten-free baguette or gluten-free crackers instead.

Roast Beef & Brie Sandwich with Tahini Sauce

2 SERVINGS 10 MINUTES

INGREDIENTS

2 tbsps Tahini

1/2 Lemon (juiced)

1 tbsp Parsley (chopped)

Sea Salt & Black Pepper (to taste)

8 ozs Sourdough Baguette (toasted)

1 cup Arugula

6 ozs Deli Roast Beef

1 oz Brie Cheese

NUTRITION

AMOUNT PER SERVING

Calories	573	Carbs	70g
Fat	17g	Protein	35g

DIRECTIONS

01   Combine the tahini, lemon juice, and parsley in a small bowl. Season the sauce with salt and pepper.

02   Cut the baguette(s) in half. Spread the sauce evenly over one side of the bun.

03   Divide the arugula, roast beef, and cheese between the baguette(s). Close the sandwich and enjoy!

NOTES

LEFTOVERS
Wrap the sandwich tightly and refrigerate for up to two days.

SERVING SIZE
One serving is equal to one sandwich.

GLUTEN-FREE
Use gluten-free bread or bun instead.

MORE FLAVOR
Add roasted red peppers. Top with fresh parsley.

NO ARUGULA   .
Use spinach, mixed greens, or lettuce instead.

Roasted Eggplant Sandwich

2 SERVINGS 40 MINUTES

INGREDIENTS

1 Eggplant (medium, sliced into 1/2 inch thick rounds)

1 tbsp Extra Virgin Olive Oil (divided)

Sea Salt & Black Pepper (to taste)

2 ozs Roasted Red Peppers

1 tsp Lemon Juice

8 ozs Sourdough Baguette (toasted)

3 ozs Mozzarella Ball (sliced)

3 tbsps Basil Leaves

NUTRITION

AMOUNT PER SERVING

Calories	580	**Carbs**	84g
Fat	18g	**Protein**	22g

DIRECTIONS

01 Preheat the oven to 400°F (205°C) and line a baking sheet with parchment paper.

02 Place the eggplant slices on the baking sheet. Toss with half of the oil and season with salt and pepper. Bake in the oven for 20 minutes or until soft and golden brown.

03 Meanwhile, in a food processor blend the roasted red pepper and lemon juice together until smooth. Season with salt and pepper.

04 Divide the roasted eggplant and roasted red pepper sauce between baguettes. Add the sliced mozzarella and basil leaves. Close the sandwich and enjoy!

NOTES

LEFTOVERS
Wrap the sandwich tightly and refrigerate for up to two days.

SERVING SIZE
One serving is equal to one sandwich.

GLUTEN-FREE
Use gluten-free bread or bun instead.

MORE FLAVOR
Add spinach, arugula, or lettuce instead. Top with fresh parsley.

MAKE IT VEGAN
Use plant-based cheese instead.

Mustard Tuna & Avocado Toast

1 SERVING 10 MINUTES

INGREDIENTS

1/2 can Tuna (drained)

1/2 tsp Ground Mustard

1 1/2 tsps Mayonnaise

Sea Salt & Black Pepper (to taste)

1/2 Avocado (medium, sliced)

1 3/4 ozs Sourdough Bread (toasted)

1/2 stalk Green Onion (sliced)

NUTRITION

AMOUNT PER SERVING

Calories	409	Carbs	33g
Fat	21g	Protein	23g

DIRECTIONS

01   Mix the tuna, ground mustard, mayonnaise, salt and pepper together.

02   Add the avocado to the toast and add the tuna on top. Garnish with green onions. Enjoy!

NOTES

LEFTOVERS
Best enjoyed immediately. Slice the avocado when ready to serve.

SERVING SIZE
One serving is half a can of tuna, half of an avocado, and one piece of sourdough bread.

MORE FLAVOR
Add capers and/or hot sauce.

GLUTEN-FREE
Use gluten-free bread.

NO GROUND MUSTARD
Omit altogether or use wasabi paste or prepared horseradish.

SOURDOUGH BREAD
One slice of sourdough bread is equal to approximately 1 3/4 oz or 50 grams.

Wasabi Tuna & Avocado Toast with Egg

1 SERVING 10 MINUTES

INGREDIENTS

1 tsp Extra Virgin Olive Oil

1 Egg

1/2 can Tuna (drained)

1 tsp Wasabi Paste

Sea Salt & Black Pepper (to taste)

1/2 Avocado (medium, sliced)

1 3/4 ozs Sourdough Bread (toasted)

1/2 stalk Green Onion (sliced)

NUTRITION

AMOUNT PER SERVING

Calories	474	**Carbs**	34g
Fat	25g	**Protein**	29g

DIRECTIONS

01 Heat the oil in a pan over medium heat. Add the egg and cook until the whites are set and the yolk is cooked to your liking.

02 Mix the tuna, wasabi paste, salt, and pepper together.

03 Add the avocado to the toast and add the tuna on top. Garnish with green onions.

04 Serve the toast with the egg and enjoy!

NOTES

LEFTOVERS
Best enjoyed immediately. Slice the avocado when ready to serve.

SERVING SIZE
One serving is half a can of tuna, half of an avocado, one piece of sourdough bread and one egg.

MORE FLAVOR
Add hot sauce.

GLUTEN-FREE
Use gluten-free bread.

NO WASABI PASTE
Use mustard powder or prepared horseradish instead.

Strawberries & Toast Assorted Snack Plate

1 SERVING 5 MINUTES

INGREDIENTS

1 tsp Butter

1 3/4 ozs Sourdough Bread (toasted)

1 Carrot (small, cut into sticks)

1 oz Salami, Mild

1 oz Cheddar Cheese (sliced)

1/2 cup Strawberries

NUTRITION

AMOUNT PER SERVING

Calories	416	Carbs	37g
Fat	21g	Protein	19g

DIRECTIONS

01   Add the butter to the toast. Assemble all of the ingredients onto a plate and enjoy!

NOTES

LEFTOVERS
Best enjoyed immediately. Refrigerate the ingredients for up to three days. Slice the bread and toast just before serving.

SOURDOUGH BREAD
One slice of sourdough bread is equal to approximately 1 3/4 oz or 50 grams.

Guacamole & Banana Pepper Toast

1 SERVING 5 MINUTES

INGREDIENTS

3 tbsps Guacamole

1 3/4 ozs Sourdough Bread (toasted)

1 oz Pickled Banana Peppers (hot)

NUTRITION

AMOUNT PER SERVING

Calories	203	Carbs	30g
Fat	6g	Protein	6g

DIRECTIONS

01 Spread the guacamole onto the toasted bread and top with pickled banana peppers. Enjoy!

NOTES

LEFTOVERS
Best enjoyed fresh.

ADDITIONAL TOPPINGS
Fresh or pickled sliced onion, fresh parsley, and/or cilantro.

GLUTEN-FREE
Use gluten-free bread.

SOURDOUGH BREAD
One slice of sourdough bread is equal to approximately 1 3/4 oz or 50 grams.

Roasted Tomato & Ricotta Toast

2 SERVINGS 30 MINUTES

INGREDIENTS

2 cups Cherry Tomatoes (halved)

1 tbsp Extra Virgin Olive Oil

1 tbsp Fennel Seed (crushed)

Sea Salt & Black Pepper (to taste)

1 cup Ricotta Cheese

3 1/2 ozs Sourdough Bread (sliced, toasted)

NUTRITION

AMOUNT PER SERVING

Calories	407	Carbs	40g
Fat	20g	Protein	16g

DIRECTIONS

01 Preheat the oven to 425°F (220°C).

02 In a bowl, gently mix together the tomatoes, oil, and fennel seeds. Season with salt and pepper.

03 Place the tomatoes cut side down into a baking dish. Cook in the oven for 15 to 20 minutes or until wilted and starting to brown.

04 Spread the ricotta onto a slice of bread and season with salt and pepper. Top with the tomatoes. Enjoy!

NOTES

LEFTOVERS
Best enjoyed fresh. Refrigerate all ingredients separately in an airtight container for up to four days.

SERVING SIZE
One serving is approximately 1/2 cup of roasted tomatoes, 1/2 cup of ricotta and one slice of bread.

ADDITIONAL TOPPINGS
Parsley and/or chives.

GLUTEN-FREE
Use gluten-free bread.

SOURDOUGH BREAD
One slice of sourdough bread is equal to approximately 1 3/4 oz or 50 grams.

Stuffing Bites

6 SERVINGS 30 MINUTES

INGREDIENTS

5 1/4 ozs Sourdough Bread (broken into pieces)
1 Egg (large)
2 tbsps Dried Unsweetened Cranberries
1 tsp Dried Rosemary
1 tsp Dried Thyme
1/2 tsp Sea Salt
1/3 cup Pecans
1 tbsp Extra Virgin Olive Oil

NUTRITION

AMOUNT PER SERVING

Calories	141	**Carbs**	15g
Fat	7g	**Protein**	4g

DIRECTIONS

01 Preheat oven to 375°F (190°C). Line a baking sheet with parchment paper.

02 Add all of the ingredients to a food processor and process until you get a coarse texture.

03 Use a teaspoon to scoop out the mixture and roll into balls. Place them on the prepared baking sheet.

04 Bake for 15 to 20 minutes or until the stuffing bites have browned lightly. Enjoy!

NOTES

LEFTOVERS
Refrigerate in an airtight container for up to three days.
SERVING SIZE
One serving is two stuffing bites.
GLUTEN-FREE
Use gluten-free bread.

Pumpkin French Toast

3 SERVINGS 15 MINUTES

INGREDIENTS

2 Egg (whisked)

1/4 cup Pureed Pumpkin

2 tbsps Unsweetened Almond Milk

1/3 cup Maple Syrup (divided)

1 tsp Cinnamon

5 1/4 ozs Sourdough Bread

1 tsp Coconut Oil

NUTRITION

AMOUNT PER SERVING

Calories	282	**Carbs**	49g
Fat	5g	**Protein**	9g

DIRECTIONS

01 Add the eggs, pureed pumpkin, milk, 1/3 of the maple syrup, and cinnamon to a large bowl. Stir until well combined.

02 Dip each piece of bread into the mixture, coating evenly on both sides.

03 Heat the oil in a pan over medium-high heat. Place the bread in the pan, working in batches if needed, for about two minutes per side, or until browned and cooked through.

04 Divide onto plates and top with the remaining maple syrup. Enjoy!

NOTES

LEFTOVERS
Best enjoyed immediately.

SERVING SIZE
One serving is one piece of toast.

NO ALMOND MILK
Use milk of choice.

ADDITIONAL TOPPINGS
Top with berries, sliced banana, pumpkin seeds, shredded coconut, and/or coconut butter.

GLUTEN-FREE
Use gluten-free bread.

NO COCONUT OIL
Use butter instead.

SOURDOUGH BREAD
One slice of sourdough bread is equal to approximately 1 3/4 oz or 50 grams.

Peanut Butter & Apple Toast

1 SERVING 5 MINUTES

INGREDIENTS

2 tbsps All Natural Peanut Butter

1 3/4 ozs Sourdough Bread (toasted)

1/2 Apple (thinly sliced)

1/8 tsp Cinnamon

1/2 tsp Raw Honey

NUTRITION

AMOUNT PER SERVING

Calories	375	Carbs	47g
Fat	17g	Protein	12g

DIRECTIONS

01   Spread the peanut butter onto the toast and top with apple, cinnamon, and honey. Enjoy!

NOTES

LEFTOVERS
Best enjoyed immediately.

SERVING SIZE
One serving is equal to one slice of toast with toppings.

ADDITIONAL TOPPINGS
Add hemp seeds.

GLUTEN-FREE
Use gluten-free bread instead.

NUT-FREE
Use sunflower seed butter or pumpkin seed butter instead.

SOURDOUGH BREAD
One slice of sourdough bread is equal to approximately 1 3/4 oz or 50 grams.

Pressure Cooker Sourdough French Toast

3 SERVINGS 45 MINUTES

INGREDIENTS

1 tsp Avocado Oil

1/2 cup Water

1 cup Unsweetened Almond Milk

1 tsp Vanilla Extract

2 Egg

9 3/4 ozs Sourdough Bread (broken into chunks)

2 tbsps Maple Syrup

NUTRITION

AMOUNT PER SERVING

Calories	340	**Carbs**	54g
Fat	6g	**Protein**	13g

DIRECTIONS

01 Brush the oil all over the inside of a glass bowl. The size of the bowl should sit on top of the metal trivet, not too snug to the sides of the pressure cooker (we used an eight inch bowl). Add the metal trivet to the pressure cooker, and then add the water.

02 In a separate large bowl, add the almond milk, vanilla extract, and eggs. Whisk well to combine. Add the bread to the bowl and mix well so that the bread soaks up the egg mixture.

03 Pour the bread mixture into the glass bowl and set it in the pressure cooker on the metal trivet. Set the pressure cooker to "sealing" and cook on high for 35 minutes.

04 Once the pressure cooker is done, manually release the pressure. Remove the bowl carefully and let sit for five minutes.

05 Divide the French toast evenly between plates, add maple syrup, and enjoy!

NOTES

LEFTOVERS
Refrigerate in an airtight container for up to three days.

SERVING SIZE
One serving is approximately 1 1/2 cups of French toast. This recipe was tested to make three servings. Due to the nature of pressure cookers, we don't recommend scaling this recipe up or down.

MORE FLAVOR
Add cinnamon, maple syrup, and/or pumpkin spice to the egg mixture before cooking.

ADDITIONAL TOPPINGS
Chopped pecans, walnuts, and/or yogurt.

Pressure Cooker Leek Soup with Cheese Toast

4 SERVINGS 25 MINUTES

INGREDIENTS

3 Leeks (large, sliced)

2 tbsps Butter

1 tbsp Thyme (fresh)

1 1/2 tsps Tamari

1 1/2 tsps White Wine Vinegar

1 1/2 tsps Worcestershire Sauce

3 1/2 cups Vegetable Broth, Low Sodium

3 ozs Sourdough Baguette (sliced)

2 ozs Cheddar Cheese (sliced)

NUTRITION

AMOUNT PER SERVING

Calories	221	**Carbs**	25g
Fat	11g	**Protein**	6g

DIRECTIONS

01 Turn the pressure cooker to "sauté" mode. Once hot, add the leeks and butter. Sauté for three to five minutes, or until softened.

02 Stir in the thyme, tamari, vinegar, and Worcestershire sauce. Add the broth.

03 Close the lid and set to "sealing". Press manual/pressure cooker and cook for eight minutes on high pressure. Once it is done, release the pressure manually. Remove the lid carefully.

04 Turn on the broiler on your oven or toaster oven. Ladle the soup into ovenproof bowls. Top with the baguette slices and place the cheese over the top. Broil for about two minutes or until the cheese is bubbly and golden. Enjoy!

NOTES

LEFTOVERS
Refrigerate in an airtight container for up to four days or freeze for up to three months. Toast is best enjoyed fresh.

SERVING SIZE
One serving is approximately 1 1/4 cups.

GLUTEN-FREE
Use gluten-free bread.

DAIRY-FREE
Use olive oil instead of butter and dairy-free cheese.

Pumpkin & Walnut French Toast Casserole

6 SERVINGS 50 MINUTES

INGREDIENTS

1 2/3 cups Pureed Pumpkin

2 Egg

1 cup Unsweetened Almond Milk

1/4 cup Maple Syrup (plus more for serving)

1 tsp Vanilla Extract

1 tsp Cinnamon

12 2/3 ozs Sourdough Bread (broken into pieces)

1/3 cup Walnuts (chopped)

NUTRITION

AMOUNT PER SERVING

Calories	283	**Carbs**	45g
Fat	7g	**Protein**	10g

DIRECTIONS

01   Preheat the oven to 375°F (190°C). Grease a baking dish.

02   In a large bowl, add the pumpkin, eggs, milk, maple syrup, vanilla extract, and cinnamon. Whisk until well combined. Add the bread and coat it well in the egg mixture so that it absorbs it as much as possible.

03   Add the bread mixture to the baking dish and top with walnuts. Bake for 40 minutes or until the bread is spongey and slightly crusty around the edges and on top.

04   Serve with additional maple syrup if desired and enjoy!

NOTES

LEFTOVERS
Refrigerate in an airtight container for up to three days.

SERVING SIZE
A 10.5 x 7.5-inch (27 x 19 cm) baking dish was used to make six servings. One serving is one piece.

MORE FLAVOR
Add pumpkin spice.

ADDITIONAL TOPPINGS
Whipped cream or yogurt.

GLUTEN-FREE
Use gluten-free bread.

SOURDOUGH CASSEROLE
One slice of sourdough bread is equal to approximately 1 3/4 oz or 50 grams.

Apple & Brie Crostini

2 SERVINGS 5 MINUTES

INGREDIENTS

1/2 Green Apple (sliced)

3 ozs Brie Cheese (sliced)

2 ozs Sourdough Baguette (sliced, toasted)

2 tsps Raw Honey

NUTRITION

AMOUNT PER SERVING

Calories	266	Carbs	28g
Fat	12g	Protein	11g

DIRECTIONS

01   Arrange the sliced apple and brie cheese on top of the toasted baguette. Drizzle the honey on top and enjoy!

NOTES

LEFTOVERS
Refrigerate in an airtight container for up to two days.

SERVING SIZE
One serving is equal to approximately three crostinis.

MORE FLAVOR
Add chili flakes on top.

GLUTEN-FREE
Use a gluten-free baguette instead.

Whipped Ricotta & Pesto Toast

2 SERVINGS 10 MINUTES

INGREDIENTS

2/3 cup Ricotta Cheese

1/2 Lemon (medium, juiced, zested)

Sea Salt & Black Pepper (to taste)

3 1/2 ozs Sourdough Bread (sliced, toasted)

2 tbsps Pesto

1/2 tsp Chili Flakes

NUTRITION

AMOUNT PER SERVING

Calories	317	Carbs	32g
Fat	14g	Protein	13g

DIRECTIONS

01 In a food processor, add the ricotta, lemon juice, lemon zest, salt, and pepper. Blend until smooth.

02 Spread the whipped ricotta on top of the toasted bread. Spoon the pesto on top and sprinkle with chili flakes. Enjoy!

NOTES

LEFTOVERS
Refrigerate the whipped ricotta in an airtight container for up to three days. Assemble just before serving.

SERVING SIZE
One serving is equal to one toast.

GLUTEN-FREE
Use gluten-free bread instead.

SOURDOUGH BREAD
One slice of sourdough bread is equal to approximately 1 3/4 oz or 50 grams.

Roasted Strawberries & Feta on Toast

2 SERVINGS 15 MINUTES

INGREDIENTS

1 1/2 cups Strawberries (chopped)

1 tsp Extra Virgin Olive Oil

2 tsps Raw Honey

3 1/2 ozs Sourdough Bread (sliced, toasted)

1/4 cup Feta Cheese (crumbled)

NUTRITION

AMOUNT PER SERVING

Calories	248	**Carbs**	39g
Fat	7g	**Protein**	8g

DIRECTIONS

01 Preheat the oven to 375°F (190°C). Place the strawberries on a rimmed baking sheet. Drizzle with oil and honey and toss to combine.

02 Cook the strawberries in the oven for 10 to 12 minutes or until slightly soft.

03 Top the toasted bread with roasted strawberries and feta cheese. Enjoy!

NOTES

LEFTOVERS
Refrigerate the roasted strawberries in an airtight container for up to three days. Assemble before serving.

SERVING SIZE
One serving is equal to one toast.

SOURDOUGH BREAD
One slice of sourdough bread is equal to approximately 1 3/4 oz or 50 grams.

ADDITIONAL TOPPINGS
Top with mint and chili flakes.

GLUTEN-FREE
Use gluten free bread instead.

Tomato & Feta Toast

1 SERVING 5 MINUTES

INGREDIENTS

1 tsp Extra Virgin Olive Oil

1 3/4 ozs Sourdough Bread (toasted)

1/4 Tomato (medium, sliced)

1/4 cup Feta Cheese (crumbled)

1 tbsp Raw Honey

1/4 tsp Chili Flakes

NUTRITION

AMOUNT PER SERVING

Calories	328	Carbs	43g
Fat	13g	Protein	10g

DIRECTIONS

01 Drizzle the oil on top of the toasted bread and top with sliced tomatoes and feta cheese. Drizzle the honey on top and season with chili flakes. Enjoy!

NOTES

LEFTOVERS
Best enjoyed fresh.

MAKE IT VEGAN
Use a plant-based cheese alternative.

MORE FLAVOR
Rub fresh garlic on the toast before adding toppings.

ADDITIONAL TOPPINGS
Fresh herbs like parsley or basil.

GLUTEN-FREE
Use gluten-free bread.

SOURDOUGH BREAD
One slice of sourdough bread is equal to approximately 1 3/4 oz or 50 grams.

Whipped Ricotta & Cherry Toast

2 SERVINGS 10 MINUTES

INGREDIENTS

2/3 cup Ricotta Cheese

1/2 Lemon (medium, juiced, zested)

Sea Salt & Black Pepper (to taste)

3 1/2 ozs Sourdough Bread (sliced, toasted)

1 cup Cherries (pits removed, halved)

1 tbsp Sesame Seeds

NUTRITION

AMOUNT PER SERVING

Calories	325	**Carbs**	44g
Fat	11g	**Protein**	13g

DIRECTIONS

01   In a food processor, add the ricotta, lemon juice, lemon zest, salt, and pepper. Blend until smooth.

02   Spread the whipped ricotta on top of the toasted bread. Arrange the cherries on top and sprinkle with sesame seeds. Enjoy!

NOTES

LEFTOVERS
Refrigerate the whipped ricotta in an airtight container for up to three days. Assemble before serving.

SERVING SIZE
One serving is equal to one toast.

ADDITIONAL TOPPINGS
Drizzle with olive oil or balsamic reduction.

GLUTEN-FREE
Use gluten-free bread instead.

SOURDOUGH BREAD
One slice of sourdough bread is equal to approximately 1 3/4 oz or 50 grams.

Avocado, Cucumber & Swiss Cheese Sandwich

1 SERVING 5 MINUTES

INGREDIENTS

1 oz Swiss Cheese (sliced)

1/4 Cucumber (medium, sliced)

1/2 Avocado (medium, sliced)

3 1/2 ozs Sourdough Bread (sliced, toasted)

1/4 Lemon (juiced)

1/8 tsp Sea Salt

NUTRITION

AMOUNT PER SERVING

Calories	534	**Carbs**	60g
Fat	24g	**Protein**	20g

DIRECTIONS

01 Add the swiss cheese, cucumber, and avocado to one side of the toast. Squeeze the lemon juice on top and season with salt. Close the sandwich, cut it in half, and enjoy!

NOTES

LEFTOVERS
Refrigerate in an airtight container for up to two days.

SERVING SIZE
One serving is equal to one sandwich.

MORE FLAVOR
Add tomato and microgreens.

GLUTEN-FREE
Use gluten-free bread instead.

SOURDOUGH BREAD
One slice of sourdough bread is equal to approximately 1 3/4 oz or 50 grams.

Smashed Avocado & Lima Bean Toast

2 SERVINGS 5 MINUTES

INGREDIENTS

1 Avocado (medium)

1 cup Lima Beans (cooked)

1/2 Lime (medium, juiced)

1/4 tsp Sea Salt

3 1/2 ozs Sourdough Bread (sliced, toasted)

1 cup Alfalfa Sprouts

1/4 tsp Chili Flakes

NUTRITION

AMOUNT PER SERVING

Calories	387	**Carbs**	52g
Fat	15g	**Protein**	13g

DIRECTIONS

01   In a bowl, smash the avocado until smooth. Add the lima beans to the bowl, lightly smash the beans and mix with avocado. Add the lime juice and sea salt, adjusting the seasoning to your taste.

02   Add the bean mixture to the toast. Top with alfalfa sprouts and chili flakes. Enjoy!

NOTES

LEFTOVERS
Refrigerate in an airtight container for up to two days.

SERVING SIZE
One serving is equal to one toast.

MORE FLAVOR
Add red onion and chopped tomato to the bean mixture.

GLUTEN-FREE
Use gluten-free bread instead.

SOURDOUGH BREAD
One slice of sourdough bread is equal to approximately 1 3/4 oz or 50 grams.

Sausage & Veggies with Eggs

2 SERVINGS 30 MINUTES

INGREDIENTS

7 ozs Pork Sausage

2 Tomato (quartered)

8 ozs Portobello Mushroom Caps

1 tbsp Extra Virgin Olive Oil (divided)

Sea Salt & Black Pepper (to taste)

2 Egg

3 1/2 ozs Sourdough Bread (sliced, toasted)

2 tbsps Parsley (chopped)

NUTRITION

AMOUNT PER SERVING

Calories	619	**Carbs**	34g
Fat	40g	**Protein**	28g

DIRECTIONS

01 Adjust the rack to the top position and preheat the oven to 425ºF (220ºC). Line a baking sheet with parchment paper.

02 Place the sausages on one side of the prepared baking sheet and cook for five minutes.

03 Arrange the tomatoes and the mushrooms (stem sides down) on the empty side of the baking sheet. Drizzle with half of the oil and season with salt and pepper. Return to the oven and cook until the veggies are tender and the sausages are cooked through, about 14 to 16 minutes.

04 Meanwhile, heat the remaining oil in a non-stick pan over medium-high heat. Cook the eggs until the whites are set, and the yolk is cooked to your liking. Set aside.

05 Divide the sausages, eggs, mushrooms, tomatoes, and toast between plates. Garnish with parsley and enjoy!

NOTES

LEFTOVERS
Refrigerate all ingredients separately in an airtight container for up to four days.
MORE FLAVOR
Serve with a portion of baked beans.
SOURDOUGH BREAD
One slice of sourdough bread is equal to approximately 1 3/4 oz or 50 grams.

Coconut Raspberry Strata

4 SERVINGS 35 MINUTES

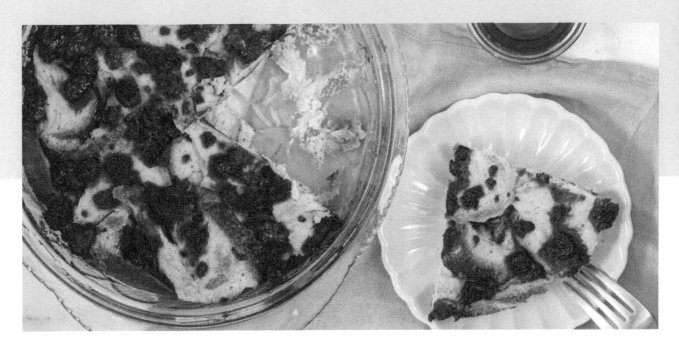

INGREDIENTS

10 1/2 ozs Sourdough Bread (torn into pieces)
1/2 cup Frozen Raspberries
3 Egg (large)
1 1/4 cups Canned Coconut Milk
1 tsp Vanilla Extract
1/2 tsp Cinnamon
1/4 cup Maple Syrup

NUTRITION

AMOUNT PER SERVING

Calories	438	Carbs	54g
Fat	17g	Protein	13g

DIRECTIONS

01 Preheat the oven to 350°F (175°C). Grease a pie dish or baking pan.

02 Add the torn bread pieces to the dish and spread the raspberries over top.

03 Whisk the eggs, milk, vanilla, and cinnamon together and pour evenly over the bread. Bake for 25 minutes or until the bread starts to brown around the edges and the strata looks spongey like French toast.

04 Cut and serve with maple syrup. Enjoy!

NOTES

LEFTOVERS
Refrigerate in an airtight container for up to three days.
SERVING SIZE
A 9 1/2-inch pie dish was used to make four servings.
MORE FLAVOR
Add seasonal fruit like peaches, blueberries, or cherries.
ADDITIONAL TOPPINGS
Chopped almonds and/or icing sugar.
GLUTEN-FREE
Use gluten-free bread.
NO COCONUT MILK
Use any milk or alternative milk.

Bacon & Cheddar Strata

4 SERVINGS 35 MINUTES

INGREDIENTS

10 1/2 ozs Sourdough Bread (torn into pieces)

3 slices Bacon (chopped)

2 1/16 ozs Cheddar Cheese (shredded)

2 stalks Green Onion (chopped)

3 Egg (large)

1 1/4 cups Cow's Milk, Whole

1/4 tsp Sea Salt

1/8 tsp Black Pepper

NUTRITION

AMOUNT PER SERVING

Calories	429	**Carbs**	41g
Fat	19g	**Protein**	21g

DIRECTIONS

01   Preheat the oven to 350°F (175°C). Grease a baking pan.

02   Add the torn bread pieces to the pan and top with the bacon, cheddar, and green onions evenly.

03   Whisk the eggs, milk, salt, and pepper together and pour over the bread evenly. Bake for 25 minutes or until the bread starts to brown around the edges and the strata looks spongey like French toast.

04   Cut and divide onto plates. Enjoy!

NOTES

LEFTOVERS
Refrigerate in an airtight container for up to three days.

PREP THE NIGHT BEFORE
You can prep this recipe the night before by following all of the same instructions but instead of baking, simply cover and refrigerate overnight.

BAKING PAN SIZE
An 8 x 8-inch square baking pan was used to make four servings.

ADDITIONAL TOPPINGS
Pickled jalapeños and/or chopped parsley. For a sweeter hot sauce, mix some maple syrup or honey and hot sauce together and drizzle over top.

GLUTEN-FREE
Use gluten-free bread instead.

DAIRY-FREE
Use dairy-free milk instead.

Lemon Strawberry French Toast Casserole

6 SERVINGS 45 MINUTES

INGREDIENTS

3 Egg

1/4 cup Butter (melted)

1/2 cup Cow's Milk, Whole

1/2 cup Maple Syrup

1 Lemon (juiced, zested)

1 tsp Vanilla Extract

1/4 tsp Sea Salt

1 1/2 lbs Sourdough Bread (sliced, halved)

2 1/2 cups Strawberries (chopped)

NUTRITION

AMOUNT PER SERVING

Calories	492	Carbs	79g
Fat	11g	Protein	15g

DIRECTIONS

01 Preheat the oven to 375°F (190°C).

02 In a large bowl, whisk together the eggs, butter, milk, maple syrup, lemon juice, lemon zest, vanilla, and salt until well combined.

03 Dip the pieces of sourdough bread into the batter, ensuring all sides are soaked. Transfer the bread into a casserole dish, filling the casserole dish completely.

04 Evenly stuff the strawberry pieces in between the slices of bread until they are all used up. Bake in the oven for 30 minutes or until starting to brown.

05 Serve with extra maple syrup and strawberries, if desired. Enjoy!

NOTES

LEFTOVERS
Refrigerate in an airtight container for up to five days.
SERVING SIZE
A 10 x 7-inch baking dish was used to make six servings.
MORE FLAVOR
Stuff the bread with ricotta cheese.
ADDITIONAL TOPPINGS
Chocolate chips, whipped cream, additional fresh fruit.
GLUTEN-FREE
Use gluten-free bread.
DAIRY-FREE
Use vegan butter and milk instead.

Bread & Butter with Radishes

2 SERVINGS 10 MINUTES

INGREDIENTS

2 tbsps Butter (unsalted, at room temperature)

3 1/2 ozs Sourdough Bread (sliced)

1/2 cup Radishes (thinly sliced)

Sea Salt & Black Pepper (to taste)

1 1/2 tsps Chives (chopped)

NUTRITION

AMOUNT PER SERVING

Calories	231	Carbs	25g
Fat	12g	Protein	5g

DIRECTIONS

01   Spread the butter onto each slice of bread. Top with the radishes.

02   Season with salt, pepper, and chives. Enjoy!

NOTES

LEFTOVERS
Best enjoyed immediately.

SERVING SIZE
One serving is equal to one slice.

Green Beans, Bacon & Eggs

1 SERVING 15 MINUTES

INGREDIENTS

2 slices Bacon

1 Egg

1/8 tsp Sea Salt

1 cup Green Beans (trimmed)

1 3/4 ozs Sourdough Bread (toasted)

NUTRITION

AMOUNT PER SERVING

Calories	447	Carbs	31g
Fat	26g	Protein	21g

DIRECTIONS

01 Heat a pan over medium-high heat and add the bacon. Cook until browned and crispy, about two to three minutes per side. Transfer the bacon to a paper towel-lined plate, leaving a small amount of bacon grease in the pan.

02 Add the egg to the pan and cook until the whites are set and the yolks are cooked to your liking. Season with half of the salt and place it onto the toast.

03 Add the green beans to the pan and sauté for two to three minutes or until tender-crisp. Season with the remaining salt. Enjoy!

NOTES

LEFTOVERS
Best enjoyed immediately.

MORE FLAVOR
Season the egg with garlic powder, paprika, and/or cumin.

GLUTEN-FREE
Use gluten-free bread instead.

SOURDOUGH BREAD
One slice of sourdough bread is equal to approximately 1 3/4 oz or 50 grams.

Whipped Ricotta & Butternut Squash Crostini

4 SERVINGS 30 MINUTES

INGREDIENTS

1 1/2 cups Butternut Squash (seeds removed, cubed)

1 1/2 tsps Extra Virgin Olive Oil

Sea Salt & Black Pepper (to taste)

1/2 cup Ricotta Cheese

1/2 Lemon (medium, juiced, zested)

4 ozs Sourdough Baguette (sliced, toasted)

NUTRITION

AMOUNT PER SERVING

Calories	166	Carbs	25g
Fat	5g	Protein	5g

DIRECTIONS

01 Preheat the oven to 425°F (220°C) and line a baking sheet with parchment paper.

02 Add the butternut squash to the baking sheet and toss with oil, salt, and pepper. Bake in the oven for 20 to 25 minutes or until golden brown.

03 Meanwhile, in a blender add the ricotta, lemon juice, lemon zest, salt, and pepper. Blend until smooth and adjust the seasoning to your taste.

04 Spread the whipped ricotta onto the sliced baguettes. Top with roasted butternut squash and enjoy!

NOTES

LEFTOVERS
Best enjoyed immediately. Refrigerate the components in separate containers for up to three days.

SERVING SIZE
One serving is approximately two to three crostinis.

ADDITIONAL TOPPINGS
Top with fresh herbs and chili flakes.

GLUTEN-FREE
Use a gluten-free baguette instead.

Edamame & Tahini on Toast

2 SERVINGS 10 MINUTES

INGREDIENTS

3 2/3 ozs Frozen Edamame

1 1/2 tbsps Tahini

2 tbsps Water

1/2 Lemon (juiced, zested)

Sea Salt & Black Pepper (to taste)

2 slices Sourdough Bread (toasted)

2 tbsps Cilantro

1/2 oz Pickled Red Onions

1/2 tsp Chili Flakes

NUTRITION

AMOUNT PER SERVING

Calories	191	Carbs	20g
Fat	10g	Protein	9g

DIRECTIONS

01   Add the edamame, tahini, water, lemon juice, lemon zest, salt, and pepper to a blender or food processor. Blend until smooth, adding more water if the mixture seems too dry. Adjust the seasoning to your taste.

02   Spread the edamame mixture over the toasted bread. Top with cilantro and pickled red onion. Sprinkle some chili flakes on top and enjoy!

NOTES

LEFTOVERS
Refrigerate the edamame mixture in an airtight container for up to three days. Assemble before serving.

SERVING SIZE
One serving is equal to one piece of toast.

NO PICKLED RED ONION
Omit or use red onion instead.

Harissa Shrimp & White Beans

2 SERVINGS 20 MINUTES

INGREDIENTS

1 tsp Extra Virgin Olive Oil

1 cup Diced Tomatoes (from the can, with the juices)

1 1/2 tbsps Harissa

1/2 Lemon (juiced, zested)

1 cup White Navy Beans (cooked, rinsed)

10 ozs Shrimp (peeled, deveined)

Sea Salt & Black Pepper (to taste)

1 tbsp Parsley (chopped)

3 1/2 ozs Sourdough Bread (toasted)

NUTRITION

AMOUNT PER SERVING

Calories	421	Carbs	53g
Fat	4g	Protein	42g

DIRECTIONS

01 Warm the oil in a skillet over medium heat. Add the diced tomatoes, harissa paste, and lemon zest. Stir and let it simmer for about five minutes.

02 Add the beans to the skillet, stirring and simmering for another five minutes. Add the shrimp to the pan and season with salt and pepper. Cover the pan with a lid and cook for another five minutes or until the shrimp is cooked through.

03 Top with lemon juice and parsley. Serve with toasted bread and enjoy!

NOTES

LEFTOVERS
Refrigerate in an airtight container for up to two days.

SERVING SIZE
One serving is equal to approximately 1 1/2 cups.

NO HARISSA
Use tomato paste, paprika, and chili flakes instead.

MORE FLAVOR
Add garlic, onion, and/or bell pepper.

GLUTEN-FREE
Use gluten-free bread instead.

SOURDOUGH BREAD
One slice of sourdough bread is equal to approximately 1 3/4 oz or 50 grams.

Vegan Cheese Melt with Tomato & Basil Pesto

4 SERVINGS 15 MINUTES

INGREDIENTS

2 1/2 ozs Cashews (soaked for 1 hour then drained)

8 fl ozs Water (hot)

1 1/2 tbsps Apple Cider Vinegar (divided)

1 tbsp Nutritional Yeast

1/4 tsp Garlic Powder

2 1/2 tbsps Tapioca Flour

1 tsp Sea Salt (divided)

1 1/3 ozs Basil Leaves

1/2 Avocado

2 tbsps Pine Nuts

2 Garlic (cloves)

1 Tomato (medium, sliced)

8 slices Sourdough Bread (toasted)

NUTRITION

AMOUNT PER SERVING

Calories	314	**Carbs**	37g
Fat	16g	**Protein**	8g

DIRECTIONS

01 Combine cashews, hot water, 1/2 of the vinegar, nutritional yeast, garlic powder, tapioca flour and half the salt in a blender until smooth. The mixture will be watery at this point.

02 Transfer to a saucepan over medium-high heat. Whisk until creamy and sticky, about 1 minute.

03 In a food processor, make the pesto. Combine basil, avocado, pine nuts, garlic and remainder of the vinegar and salt.

04 Spread basil pesto on toast and top with tomato, vegan cheese and another slice of toast to create the sandwich. Enjoy!

NOTES

NO PINE NUTS
Use sunflower seeds or walnuts instead.

LEFTOVERS
Refrigerate leftover pesto and vegan cheese separately in air-tight containers up to 5 to 7 days.

Fig & Goat Cheese Toast

1 SERVING 5 MINUTES

INGREDIENTS

2 tbsps Goat Cheese

1 3/4 ozs Sourdough Bread (toasted)

2 Fig (sliced)

NUTRITION

AMOUNT PER SERVING

Calories	233	**Carbs**	44g
Fat	3g	**Protein**	8g

DIRECTIONS

01   Spread the goat cheese over the sourdough bread. Top with figs. Enjoy!

NOTES

LEFTOVERS
Best enjoyed immediately.

SERVING SIZE
One serving is equal to one slice of toast.

MAKE IT VEGAN
Use plant-based cheese. Use hummus instead of cheese.

MORE FLAVOR
Add chili flakes, and/or a drizzle of honey.

GLUTEN-FREE
Use gluten-free bread instead.

SOURDOUGH BREAD
One slice of sourdough bread is equal to approximately 1 3/4 oz or 50 grams.

Fig, Goat Cheese & Prosciutto Toast

1 SERVING 5 MINUTES

INGREDIENTS

2 tbsps Goat Cheese

1 3/4 ozs Sourdough Bread (toasted)

2 Fig (sliced)

1 1/2 ozs Prosciutto (thinly sliced, torn into bite sized pieces)

NUTRITION

AMOUNT PER SERVING

Calories	324	**Carbs**	44g
Fat	9g	**Protein**	18g

DIRECTIONS

01 Spread the goat cheese over the sourdough bread. Top with figs and prosciutto. Enjoy!

NOTES

LEFTOVERS
Best enjoyed fresh.

SERVING SIZE
One serving is equal to one slice of toast.

MORE FLAVOR
Add chili flakes, honey, and/or extra virgin olive oil.

GLUTEN-FREE
Use gluten-free bread instead.

DAIRY-FREE
Use dairy-free cheese. Omit the cheese and use hummus instead.

SOURDOUGH BREAD
One slice of sourdough bread is equal to approximately 1 3/4 oz or 50 grams.

Baked Salmon Sandwich

1 SERVING 20 MINUTES

INGREDIENTS

5 ozs Salmon Fillet

1/2 tsp Sea Salt

3 tbsps Unsweetened Coconut Yogurt

1 tbsp Fresh Dill (chopped)

1/4 head Green Lettuce (small, leaves separated)

1/4 Tomato (sliced)

2 slices Sourdough Bread

NUTRITION

AMOUNT PER SERVING

Calories	320	Carbs	25g
Fat	9g	Protein	34g

DIRECTIONS

01 Preheat the oven to 450°F (232°C) and line a baking sheet with parchment paper.

02 Place the salmon on the baking sheet and season with sea salt. Bake for 15 minutes, or until the salmon flakes with a fork.

03 Meanwhile, combine the coconut yogurt with dill.

04 Layer the lettuce, tomato, salmon and coconut yogurt dill sauce between the slices of bread. Enjoy!

NOTES

LEFTOVERS
Best enjoyed immediately. Refrigerate in an airtight container for up to two days.
GLUTEN-FREE
Use gluten-free bread instead.
NO COCONUT YOGURT
Use mayonnaise or greek yogurt instead.

Egg & Collard Greens on Toast

1 SERVING 15 MINUTES

INGREDIENTS

2 tsps Butter (divided)

1 Egg (large)

3/4 cup Collard Greens (chopped)

1 3/4 ozs Sourdough Bread (toasted)

1 tsp Parsley (chopped)

NUTRITION

AMOUNT PER SERVING

Calories	272	**Carbs**	26g
Fat	13g	**Protein**	12g

DIRECTIONS

01 Warm half of the butter in a pan over medium heat. Once warm, add the egg(s) to the pan and cook until the whites are set and the yolk is cooked to your liking. Set aside.

02 Add the remaining butter to the pan. Sauté the collard greens for about two to three minutes, or until cooked down.

03 Put the collard greens on the toast. Add the egg on top and garnish with the parsley. Enjoy!

NOTES

LEFTOVERS
Best enjoyed immediately. Cook the collard greens ahead of time to save on time.

SERVING SIZE
One serving is one piece of toast with toppings.

MORE FLAVOR
Add hummus to the toast.

ADDITIONAL TOPPINGS
Hot sauce, sesame seeds, and/or lemon juice.

SOURDOUGH BREAD
One slice of sourdough bread is equal to approximately 1 3/4 oz or 50 grams.

Egg, Hummus & Green Beans on Toast

1 SERVING 20 MINUTES

INGREDIENTS

1/2 cup Green Beans (trimmed)

1 tsp Butter

1 Egg

1 1/2 tbsps Hummus

1 3/4 ozs Sourdough Bread (toasted)

1 tsp Parsley (chopped)

NUTRITION

AMOUNT PER SERVING

Calories	300	**Carbs**	31g
Fat	13g	**Protein**	14g

DIRECTIONS

01 Place the green beans in a steamer basket over boiling water and cover. Steam for three to five minutes.

02 Warm the butter in a pan over medium heat. Once warm, add the egg to the pan and cook until the whites are set and the yolk is cooked to your liking.

03 Spread the hummus onto the toast. Top with the green beans and the egg. Garnish with parsley and enjoy!

NOTES

LEFTOVERS
Refrigerate in an airtight container for two days.

SERVING SIZE
One serving is one piece of toast.

MAKE IT VEGAN
Omit the egg.

ADDITIONAL TOPPINGS
Crushed chilli peppers and/or black pepper.

GLUTEN-FREE
Use gluten-free bread.

DAIRY-FREE
Use oil instead of butter.

SOURDOUGH BREAD
One slice of sourdough bread is equal to approximately 1 3/4 oz or 50 grams.

Candied Walnut, Pear & Goat Cheese Crostinis

8 SERVINGS 50 MINUTES

INGREDIENTS

14 ozs Sourdough Baguette (sliced)

2 tbsps Extra Virgin Olive Oil

2 cups Walnuts

1/3 cup Maple Syrup

1 tsp Vanilla Extract

1/4 tsp Sea Salt

1 cup Goat Cheese (soft)

2 Pear (medium, thinly sliced)

NUTRITION

AMOUNT PER SERVING

Calories	462	**Carbs**	49g
Fat	26g	**Protein**	11g

DIRECTIONS

01 Preheat the oven to 400°F (205°C). Slice the baguette and arrange the slices onto a baking sheet.

02 Drizzle the oil all over and rub it into both sides of each piece of bread. Bake for 10 to 15 minutes or until lightly golden.

03 While the bread is in the oven, heat a pan over medium heat. Once hot, add the walnuts, maple syrup, vanilla, and salt. Continuously stir until all of the walnuts are coated and the maple syrup is no longer liquid in the pan. Let them cool for 10 to 15 minutes.

04 To assemble, spread the cheese onto each piece of bread. Top with the sliced pear and walnuts. Enjoy!

NOTES

LEFTOVERS
Best enjoyed fresh. Refrigerate in an airtight container for up to three days.
SERVING SIZE
One serving is two pieces.
MAKE IT VEGAN
Use a plant-based cheese alternative.
ADDITIONAL TOPPINGS
Drizzle honey or maple syrup on top.
GLUTEN-FREE
Use gluten-free bread.

Mediterranean Hummus Toast

2 SERVINGS 10 MINUTES

INGREDIENTS

2 slices Sourdough Bread (toasted)

1 Garlic (clove, peeled)

2 1/8 ozs Hummus

2 2/3 ozs Cherry Tomatoes (halved)

1 2/3 ozs Pitted Kalamata Olives (halved)

1/2 tsp Oregano

1/2 tsp Chili Flakes

1/2 tsp Ground Sumac

1/2 tsp Sea Salt (flaky)

2 tbsps Fresh Dill (chopped)

NUTRITION

AMOUNT PER SERVING

Calories	164	Carbs	19g
Fat	8g	Protein	4g

DIRECTIONS

01   Rub garlic on both pieces of the toasted bread.

02   To assemble, place the bread on plates and top evenly with the hummus, tomatoes, olives, oregano, chili flakes, sumac, sea salt, and dill. Enjoy!

NOTES

LEFTOVERS
Best enjoyed right away.

MORE FLAVOR
Drizzle olive oil on top.

GLUTEN-FREE
Use gluten-free bread.

ADDITIONAL TOPPINGS
Fresh parsley, basil, feta cheese, goat cheese.

Halloumi & Tahini on Toast

1 SERVING 5 MINUTES

INGREDIENTS

2 ozs Halloumi (sliced)

1 tbsp Tahini

1 3/4 ozs Sourdough Bread (toasted)

1 1/2 tsps Raw Honey

1/4 tsp Chili Flakes

NUTRITION

AMOUNT PER SERVING

Calories	466	**Carbs**	36g
Fat	26g	**Protein**	21g

DIRECTIONS

01 Warm a pan over medium-high heat. Cook the halloumi slices until golden brown, about one to two minutes per side.

02 Spread the tahini over the sourdough bread. Top with halloumi, honey, and chili flakes. Enjoy!

NOTES

LEFTOVERS
Best enjoyed immediately. Refrigerate the halloumi in an airtight container for up to three days.

SERVING SIZE
One serving is equal to one slice of toast.

ADDITIONAL TOPPINGS
Add sesame seeds and flaky salt.

GLUTEN-FREE
Use gluten-free bread instead.

SOURDOUGH BREAD
One slice of sourdough bread is equal to approximately 1 3/4 oz or 50 grams.

Spinach & Tuna Grilled Cheese

1 SERVING 15 MINUTES

INGREDIENTS

1/2 can Tuna (drained and flaked)

1/4 stalk Celery (diced)

1 tsp Mayonnaise

1/4 Lemon (juiced)

Sea Salt & Black Pepper (to taste)

1/2 cup Baby Spinach

3 1/2 ozs Sourdough Bread (sliced)

1 1/16 ozs Cheddar Cheese (shredded)

1 tsp Butter

NUTRITION

AMOUNT PER SERVING

Calories	513	Carbs	50g
Fat	18g	Protein	33g

DIRECTIONS

01 Preheat a cast-iron skillet over medium-low heat.

02 In a bowl, mix together the tuna, celery, mayonnaise, and lemon juice. Season with salt and pepper.

03 Layer the spinach on top of a bread. Top with tuna mixture and cheddar cheese. Close the sandwich.

04 Add the butter to the preheated pan and place the sandwich in the skillet. Cook until lightly browned on one side, flip and cook until browned on the other side. Slice and enjoy!

NOTES

LEFTOVERS
Best enjoyed immediately or refrigerate in an airtight container for up to two days.

SERVING SIZE
One serving is equal to one sandwich.

MORE FLAVOR
Add parsley or dill.

GLUTEN-FREE
Use gluten-free bread instead.

DAIRY-FREE
Use dairy-free cheese instead.

SOURDOUGH BREAD
One slice of sourdough bread is equal to approximately 1 3/4 oz or 50 grams.

CANNED TUNA
One can of tuna is equal to 165 grams or 5.8 ounces, drained.

Salmon Avocado Sandwich

1 SERVING 10 MINUTES

INGREDIENTS

1 tsp Butter

3 1/2 ozs Sourdough Bread (sliced, toasted)

1/2 Avocado (medium, mashed)

4 ozs Canned Wild Salmon (boneless, skinless)

1 tbsp Lemon Juice

1/8 tsp Sea Salt

1/4 cup Microgreens

NUTRITION

AMOUNT PER SERVING

Calories	633	Carbs	59g
Fat	25g	Protein	42g

DIRECTIONS

01 Spread the butter onto the bread. Mix the avocado, salmon, lemon juice, and salt together. Spread it onto the bread.

02 Add the microgreens on top of the salmon mixture and close the sandwich. Enjoy!

NOTES

LEFTOVERS
Refrigerate in an airtight container for two days.

SERVING SIZE
One serving is two pieces of bread and five ounces of salmon.

ADDITIONAL TOPPINGS
Add sliced tomato, capers, and/or fresh chopped dill.

GLUTEN-FREE
Use gluten-free bread.

SOURDOUGH BREAD
One slice of sourdough bread is equal to approximately 1 3/4 oz or 50 grams.

Curried Tuna Salad Sandwich

2 SERVINGS 10 MINUTES

INGREDIENTS

1 can Tuna (drained)

2 tbsps Mayonnaise

1 stalk Green Onion (finely chopped)

1/2 stalk Celery (finely chopped)

1 1/2 tsps Pickle (sweet, finely chopped)

1/4 tsp Curry Powder

1 2/3 ozs Microgreens

4 slices Sourdough Bread

NUTRITION

AMOUNT PER SERVING

Calories	287	Carbs	25g
Fat	12g	Protein	19g

DIRECTIONS

01 In a bowl, mix the tuna with the mayonnaise, green onions, celery, pickles, and curry powder.

02 Divide the microgreens and tuna salad evenly between the bread. Close the sandwich and enjoy!

NOTES

LEFTOVERS

Refrigerate the tuna salad in an airtight container for up to three days. Assemble the sandwich the day of.

SERVING SIZE

One serving is equal to one sandwich.

MORE FLAVOR

Use lettuce or baby spinach instead of microgreens. Add walnuts and/or pumpkin seeds.

GLUTEN-FREE

Use gluten-free bread.

CANNED TUNA

One can of tuna is equal to 165 grams or 5.8 ounces, drained.

Savory French Toast with Eggs

2 SERVINGS 20 MINUTES

INGREDIENTS

2 Egg (large)

1/3 cup Whipping Cream

2 stalks Green Onion (chopped)

1/8 tsp Sea Salt

7 1/16 ozs Sourdough Bread (sliced)

1 tbsp Extra Virgin Olive Oil

2 tbsps Maple Syrup

2 tsps Hot Sauce

1 tbsp Parsley (chopped)

NUTRITION

AMOUNT PER SERVING

Calories	590	**Carbs**	64g
Fat	28g	**Protein**	17g

DIRECTIONS

01 Whisk the eggs, cream, green onions, and salt together in a large shallow bowl. Add the sliced bread and soak it to ensure it absorbs most of the egg mixture.

02 Meanwhile, heat the oil in a large pan over medium heat.

03 Add the bread to the pan and cook for two to three minutes on each side until a light brown crust forms. When the bread is cooked, set it aside in the oven to keep it warm.

04 Add the remaining egg mixture to the same pan and scramble until the eggs are cooked to your liking.

05 Mix the maple syrup and hot sauce together.

06 Divide the french toast and scrambled eggs evenly between plates. Top with the hot maple syrup mixture and parsley. Enjoy!

NOTES

LEFTOVERS
Refrigerate in an airtight container for two days.

SERVING SIZE
One serving is two pieces of bread with eggs.

ADDITIONAL TOPPINGS
Smoked salmon, chopped dill, and/or creme fraiche.

GLUTEN-FREE
Use gluten-free bread.

DAIRY-FREE
Use coconut cream instead of heavy cream.

Egg & Mushroom Toast

1 SERVING 10 MINUTES

INGREDIENTS

2 tsps Butter (divided)

4 Cremini Mushrooms (sliced)

Sea Salt & Black Pepper (to taste)

1 Egg

1 3/4 ozs Sourdough Bread (toasted)

2 tsps Parmigiano Reggiano (finely grated)

NUTRITION

AMOUNT PER SERVING

Calories	298	**Carbs**	27g
Fat	14g	**Protein**	15g

DIRECTIONS

01   Melt half of the butter in a large skillet over medium heat. Add the mushrooms and cook until softened, about five minutes. Season with salt and pepper and set aside.

02   Add the egg(s) to the same skillet. Cook until the whites are set and the yolks are cooked to your liking. Season with salt and pepper.

03   Spread the remaining butter onto the toast. Top with mushrooms, egg, and parmesan cheese. Enjoy!

NOTES

LEFTOVERS
Best enjoyed fresh.

SERVING SIZE
One serving is one slice of toast with toppings.

ADDITIONAL TOPPINGS
Chopped parsley or hot sauce.

GLUTEN-FREE
Use gluten-free bread.

DAIRY-FREE
Omit the parmesan or use nutritional yeast instead.

Asparagus Avocado Toast

1 SERVING 10 MINUTES

INGREDIENTS

1/4 tsp Extra Virgin Olive Oil

3/4 cup Asparagus (chopped, woody ends trimmed)

1/2 Avocado (medium)

1/4 Lime (juiced)

Sea Salt & Black Pepper (to taste)

1 3/4 ozs Sourdough Bread (toasted)

1 tbsp Feta Cheese (crumbled)

1/4 tsp Chili Flakes (optional)

NUTRITION

AMOUNT PER SERVING

Calories	342	Carbs	38g
Fat	18g	Protein	10g

DIRECTIONS

01 Warm the oil in a pan over medium heat. Add the asparagus and sauté for four to five minutes or until the asparagus is fork tender.

02 In a bowl, add the avocado and lime juice. Mash the avocado with a fork and season with salt and pepper.

03 Spread the avocado on top of the toast. Top with sautéed asparagus, feta cheese, and chili flakes, if using. Enjoy!

NOTES

LEFTOVERS
Best enjoyed immediately.

MAKE IT VEGAN
Omit feta cheese or use plant-based cheese instead.

ADDITIONAL TOPPINGS
Cilantro or parsley.

NO FETA CHEESE
Omit or use nutritional yeast or parmesan instead.

GLUTEN-FREE
Use gluten-free bread instead.

Pomegranate Avocado Toast

1 SERVING 5 MINUTES

INGREDIENTS

1/2 Avocado (medium)

1/4 Lime (juiced)

Sea Salt & Black Pepper (to taste)

1 3/4 ozs Sourdough Bread (toasted)

2 tbsps Pomegranate Seeds

1 tbsp Feta Cheese (crumbled)

1/4 tsp Chili Flakes (optional)

NUTRITION

AMOUNT PER SERVING

Calories	327	**Carbs**	37g
Fat	17g	**Protein**	8g

DIRECTIONS

01 In a bowl, add the avocado and lime juice. Mash the avocado with a fork and season with salt and pepper.

02 Spread the avocado on top of the toast. Top with pomegranate seeds and feta cheese. Sprinkle chili flakes on top, if using, and enjoy!

NOTES

LEFTOVERS
Best enjoyed immediately.

MAKE IT VEGAN
Omit feta cheese or use plant-based cheese instead.

ADDITIONAL TOPPINGS
Fresh cilantro or dill.

GLUTEN-FREE
Use gluten-free bread instead.

Chocolate French Toast

2 SERVINGS 20 MINUTES

INGREDIENTS

1 tsp Butter (divided)

2 Egg (whisked)

3/4 cup Oat Milk

1 tsp Cacao Powder

1 tsp Vanilla Extract

7 1/16 ozs Sourdough Bread (sliced)

3 tbsps Maple Syrup

1/2 oz Dark Chocolate (shaved)

NUTRITION

AMOUNT PER SERVING

Calories	516	**Carbs**	79g
Fat	12g	**Protein**	18g

DIRECTIONS

01 Preheat a large skillet or cast iron pan over medium heat. Lightly grease the pan with half of the butter.

02 Mix the eggs, milk, cacao powder, and vanilla extract in a large, wide bowl. Working one slice at a time, soak the bread in the egg mixture, being sure to coat the bread well.

03 Place the bread in the pan and cook for three to four minutes on each side until browned. Work in batches as needed.

04 Plate the french toast and serve with the remaining butter, maple syrup, and dark chocolate. Enjoy!

NOTES

LEFTOVERS

Refrigerate in an airtight container for up to three days. Freeze in an airtight container for up to one month.

SERVING SIZE

One serving is approximately two slices of french toast.

ADDITIONAL TOPPINGS

Top with fresh berries, hemp seeds, walnuts, and/or pecans.

GLUTEN-FREE

Use gluten-free bread.

DAIRY-FREE

Omit the butter or use vegan butter.

Prosciutto Asparagus & Soft Boiled Egg

1 SERVING 15 MINUTES

INGREDIENTS

3/4 cup Asparagus (woody ends trimmed)

1 oz Prosciutto (thinly sliced strips)

1/4 tsp Sea Salt (divided)

1 Egg

1 3/4 ozs Sourdough Bread (toasted)

NUTRITION

AMOUNT PER SERVING

Calories	276	**Carbs**	28g
Fat	8g	**Protein**	20g

DIRECTIONS

01 Preheat the oven to 425°F (220°C). Line a baking sheet with parchment paper.

02 Wrap three or four asparagus spears with prosciutto. Repeat until the asparagus and prosciutto are used up. Sprinkle the asparagus with half of the salt. Bake in the oven for 10 minutes, flipping halfway.

03 Meanwhile, bring a medium-sized pot of water to a boil and add the egg(s). Boil for six to seven minutes then immediately remove and place in icy water.

04 Once the egg(s) have cooled, peel and sprinkle it with the remaining salt. Serve it with bread and roasted asparagus. Enjoy!

NOTES

LEFTOVERS
Best enjoyed immediately. Boil the eggs in advance and keep them in their shell until ready to enjoy.

MORE FLAVOR
Serve with mixed green salad.

ADDITIONAL TOPPINGS
Add chili flakes.

GLUTEN-FREE
Use gluten-free bread instead.

Avocado Toast with a Poached Egg

1 SERVING 15 MINUTES

INGREDIENTS

1 slice Bread

1/2 Avocado

Sea Salt & Black Pepper (to taste)

1 Egg

1 tbsp Apple Cider Vinegar

1/8 tsp Sea Salt

NUTRITION

AMOUNT PER SERVING

Calories	313	**Carbs**	21g
Fat	22g	**Protein**	10g

DIRECTIONS

01 Toast bread.

02 Cut avocado in half, remove the pit and cut into fine slices. Layer avocado on the toast, mash with a fork and season with a bit of sea salt and black pepper.

03 Crack your egg into a bowl.

04 Bring a pot of water to a rolling boil on your stovetop. Add sea salt and vinegar. Begin stirring your water with a spoon to create a whirlpool. Carefully add your egg into the whirlpool. Cook for 3 to 4 minutes then use a slotted spoon to carefully remove from the poached egg onto a plate lined with paper towel to soak up the excess liquid.

05 Transfer the egg to the top of your toast and season again with sea salt and pepper. Enjoy!

Cucumber & Vegan Herbed Ricotta Toast

4 SERVINGS 10 MINUTES

INGREDIENTS

2 cups Cashews (soaked for 1 hour and drained)

1/4 cup Unsweetened Almond Milk

2 Garlic (cloves, minced)

1 tbsp Chives (chopped)

2 tbsps Basil Leaves (chopped)

1 1/2 tsps Maple Syrup

3 tbsps Apple Cider Vinegar

1/4 tsp Black Pepper

1/2 tsp Sea Salt

4 slices Bread

1/2 Cucumber (sliced)

NUTRITION

AMOUNT PER SERVING

Calories	492	**Carbs**	39g
Fat	34g	**Protein**	13g

DIRECTIONS

01 Combine cashews, almond milk, garlic, chives, basil, maple syrup, vinegar, black pepper and salt in a food processor or blender. Blend until smooth.

02 Spread vegan ricotta mixture onto toast and top with cucumber slices, with additional salt and pepper (to taste, optional).

NOTES

NO CHIVES OR BASIL
Use dried herbs or any fresh herbs you have on hand.

NO CUCUMBER
Top with slices of tomato, red onion, and/or fresh herbs.

NO APPLE CIDER VINEGAR
Use lemon juice instead.

TOO RUNNY OR TOO THICK
Add more cashews to the ricotta mixture if too runny, or more almond milk if too thick.

STORAGE
Refrigerate vegan ricotta mixture in air-tight container up to 3-5 days.

Bacon & Olive Sourdough Strata

6 SERVINGS 55 MINUTES

INGREDIENTS

11 ozs Sourdough Bread (cubed)

5 slices Bacon (chopped)

1/2 cup Sun Dried Tomatoes (from the jar, drained, and chopped)

1/2 cup Black Olives (sliced)

1/2 cup Red Onion (diced)

1/3 cup Parsley (chopped)

4 ozs Cheddar Cheese (shredded)

10 Egg

1/2 cup Cow's Milk, Whole

Sea Salt & Black Pepper (to taste)

NUTRITION

AMOUNT PER SERVING

Calories	461	**Carbs**	32g
Fat	25g	**Protein**	25g

DIRECTIONS

01   Preheat the oven to 400°F (205°C).

02   Fill a casserole dish with the bread, bacon, sun dried tomatoes, black olives, red onion, parsley, and cheese.

03   In a large mixing bowl, whisk together the eggs, milk, salt, and pepper to taste. Pour into the casserole dish, then mix well to combine.

04   Bake in the oven for 30 minutes, covered. Remove the lid or tinfoil and bake for another 10 minutes or until cooked through.

05   Slice, serve, and enjoy!

NOTES

LEFTOVERS
Refrigerate in an airtight container for up to five days. Freeze for up to three months.

SERVING SIZE
A 10 x 7-inch baking dish was used to make six servings. Once serving is one piece.

MORE FLAVOR
Add garlic, basil, and oregano.

ADDITIONAL TOPPINGS
Red or green bell peppers, spinach, mushrooms, artichoke hearts, and/or feta cheese.

GLUTEN-FREE
Use gluten-free bread.

DAIRY-FREE
Use dairy-free milk and cheese.

Tuna & Tomato on Toast

1 SERVING 5 MINUTES

INGREDIENTS

1/2 can Tuna (drained and flaked)

1/4 cup Cherry Tomatoes (halved)

1 3/4 ozs Sourdough Bread (toasted)

1/8 tsp Sea Salt (to taste)

1/4 cup Microgreens

1/4 Lemon (juiced)

NUTRITION

AMOUNT PER SERVING

Calories	212	Carbs	28g
Fat	1g	Protein	22g

DIRECTIONS

01 Arrange the tuna and cherry tomatoes on top of the toast and sprinkle salt on top.

02 Top with microgreens and lemon juice. Enjoy!

NOTES

LEFTOVERS
Best enjoyed immediately.

NO MICROGREENS
Use spinach or arugula instead.

GLUTEN-FREE
Use a gluten-free bread instead.

MORE FLAVOR
Mix the tuna with yogurt or mayonnaise and mustard.

CANNED TUNA
One can of tuna is equal to 165 grams or 5.8 ounces, drained.

Kiwi, Almonds & Cream Cheese Toast

1 SERVING 5 MINUTES

INGREDIENTS

1/4 cup Cream Cheese, Regular (at room temperature)

1 3/4 ozs Sourdough Bread (toasted)

1 Kiwi (peeled, sliced)

1 tbsp Almonds (roasted, chopped)

1 tsp Honey

NUTRITION

AMOUNT PER SERVING

Calories	416	Carbs	44g
Fat	22g	Protein	12g

DIRECTIONS

01 Spread the cream cheese over the toast. Top with the kiwi slices, almonds, and honey. Enjoy!

NOTES

LEFTOVERS
For best results, enjoy freshly made. Refrigerate ingredients in separate containers for up to three days.

SERVING SIZE
One serving is one slice of toast.

GLUTEN-FREE
Use gluten-free bread.

DAIRY-FREE
Use vegan cream cheese.

Egg & Spinach on Toast

1 SERVING 15 MINUTES

INGREDIENTS

1 Egg
1/2 tsp Extra Virgin Olive Oil
2 Garlic (cloves, sliced)
1/2 tsp Chili Flakes
1 1/3 cups Baby Spinach
1/8 tsp Sea Salt (to taste)
1 3/4 ozs Sourdough Bread (toasted)

NUTRITION

AMOUNT PER SERVING

Calories	234	Carbs	28g
Fat	7g	Protein	13g

DIRECTIONS

01   Bring a pot of water to a boil. Once boiling, reduce the heat slightly and add the egg. Cook for 6 1/2 minutes for a soft-boiled egg. Once the egg is done, add to a bowl of ice water and set aside.

02   Meanwhile, heat the oil in a skillet over medium heat. Add garlic and chili flakes and sauté for a minute. Add spinach and cook for two to three minutes or until soft. Season with salt and pepper.

03   Add the spinach to the toast. Peel the egg, slice it in half, and place it on top of the spinach. Enjoy!

NOTES

LEFTOVERS
Best enjoyed immediately.
MORE FLAVOR
Add onion and tomatoes.
GLUTEN-FREE
Use gluten-free bread instead.

Brie, Prosciutto & Pear Sandwich

1 SERVING 10 MINUTES

INGREDIENTS

1 tsp Dijon Mustard

3 1/2 ozs Sourdough Bread (toasted)

1 oz Brie Cheese (sliced)

2 ozs Prosciutto

1/2 Pear (sliced)

1/2 tsp Extra Virgin Olive Oil

NUTRITION

AMOUNT PER SERVING

Calories	540	**Carbs**	61g
Fat	17g	**Protein**	30g

DIRECTIONS

01 Spread the mustard onto the toast. Layer the brie, prosciutto, and pear on one slice of bread. Drizzle the oil on top of the sandwich and top with the other piece of bread. Enjoy!

NOTES

LEFTOVERS
Refrigerate in an airtight container for up to three days.

SERVING SIZE
One serving is one sandwich.

MORE FLAVOR
Add arugula or fresh basil leaves.

GLUTEN-FREE
Use gluten-free bread.

DAIRY-FREE
Omit the brie cheese.

SOURDOUGH BREAD
One slice of sourdough bread is equal to approximately 1 3/4 oz or 50 grams.

Black Eyed Peas & Mushrooms on Toast

2 SERVINGS 20 MINUTES

INGREDIENTS

1/2 cup Shiitake Mushrooms (stem removed, chopped)

1/4 cup Vegetable Broth (divided)

1 cup Black Eyed Peas (cooked, drained and rinsed)

1 tsp Smoked Paprika

Sea Salt & Black Pepper (to taste)

3 1/2 ozs Sourdough Bread (toasted)

1 tbsp Parsley (chopped)

1/2 Lemon (juiced)

NUTRITION

AMOUNT PER SERVING

Calories	266	**Carbs**	51g
Fat	1g	**Protein**	13g

DIRECTIONS

01 Warm the skillet over medium heat. Add the mushrooms to the pan along with a splash of broth. Cook and stir occasionally for about three minutes or until mushrooms are cooked.

02 Add the black eyed peas, paprika, and the remaining broth to the pan. Bring to boil then reduce the heat down to simmer. Let simmer for about five minutes, then use a fork and smash some of the peas into the pan.

03 Season with salt and pepper and pour the beans over the toast.

04 Top with parsley and squeeze some lemon juice on top. Enjoy!

NOTES

LEFTOVERS
Refrigerate the beans and mushroom mixture in an airtight container for up to three days. Assemble before serving.

SERVING SIZE
One serving is equal to one piece of toast with 2/3 cup bean mixture.

MORE FLAVOR
Add red onion, cumin, and chili flakes.

GLUTEN-FREE
Use gluten free bread instead.

SOURDOUGH BREAD
One slice of sourdough bread is equal to approximately 1 3/4 oz or 50 grams.

NO SHIITAKE MUSHROOMS
Use any other mushroom instead.

Turkey & Provolone Grilled Cheese

1 SERVING 10 MINUTES

INGREDIENTS

1 1/2 tbsps Pesto

3 1/2 ozs Sourdough Bread

1/2 cup Arugula

3 1/2 ozs Sliced Turkey Breast

1 1/2 ozs Provolone Cheese (sliced)

1/2 tsp Extra Virgin Olive Oil

NUTRITION

AMOUNT PER SERVING

Calories	624	**Carbs**	54g
Fat	26g	**Protein**	38g

DIRECTIONS

01   Spread the pesto onto both slices of bread. Top with arugula, sliced turkey, and cheese. Close the sandwich.

02   Heat a cast iron skillet over medium-low heat. Once hot, add the oil and place the sandwich in the skillet. Cook until lightly browned on one side, flip and cook the other side.

03   Remove from the skillet. Slice and enjoy!

NOTES

LEFTOVERS
Best enjoyed immediately or refrigerate in an airtight container for up to two days.

SERVING SIZE
One serving is equal to one sandwich.

NO ARUGULA
Use baby spinach instead.

GLUTEN-FREE
Use gluten-free bread instead.

DAIRY-FREE
Use dairy-free cheese instead.

SOURDOUGH BREAD
One slice of sourdough bread is equal to approximately 1 3/4 oz or 50 grams.

Chicken & Celery Root Slaw Sandwich

4 SERVINGS 25 MINUTES

INGREDIENTS

1 tsp Avocado Oil

1 lb Chicken Breast

2 cups Celery Root (shredded)

1 Green Apple (large, shredded)

3 ozs Pickled Red Onions

2 tbsps Mayonnaise

1 tsp Raw Honey

Sea Salt & Black Pepper (to taste)

2 cups Arugula

14 ozs Sourdough Bread

NUTRITION

AMOUNT PER SERVING

Calories	513	**Carbs**	65g
Fat	11g	**Protein**	37g

DIRECTIONS

01   Warm the oil in a pan over medium heat and add the chicken breasts. Add a little water to the pan and cover with a lid. Cook for 15 to 20 minutes, flipping halfway through, or until cooked through.

02   In a mixing bowl, combine the shredded celery root, apple, onion, mayonnaise, honey, salt, and pepper to taste. Mix well to combine.

03   Slice the cooked chicken breast into thin pieces. Divide the arugula, coleslaw, and chicken evenly between the bread slices. Cut in half if desired and enjoy!

NOTES

LEFTOVERS
Best enjoyed immediately. Ingredients can be kept separately in an airtight container in the fridge for up to three days.

SERVING SIZE
One serving is equal to one sandwich.

MAKE IT VEGAN
Use tofu or tempeh instead of chicken. Use vegan mayonnaise instead of mayonnaise.

ADDITIONAL TOPPINGS
Cheese and/or fresh herbs.

GLUTEN-FREE
Use gluten-free bread.

SOURDOUGH BREAD
One slice of sourdough bread is equal to approximately 1 3/4 oz or 50 grams.

Smoked Salmon Avocado Toast

1 SERVING 5 MINUTES

INGREDIENTS

1/2 Avocado

1 slice Bread (toasted)

1 1/2 ozs Smoked Salmon (cut into bite-sized pieces)

1/8 Yellow Onion (thinly sliced)

1/2 tsp Capers

1 1/2 tsps Fresh Dill (chopped)

1/4 tsp Lemon Juice

NUTRITION

AMOUNT PER SERVING

Calories	294	**Carbs**	22g
Fat	19g	**Protein**	12g

DIRECTIONS

01 Mash the avocado onto your toast. Next, add the smoked salmon, yellow onion, capers, dill and lemon juice. Enjoy!

NOTES

NO YELLOW ONION
Use red or green onions instead.

NO BREAD
Use a large cracker or flatbread.

GLUTEN-FREE
Use gluten-free toast or crackers.

NO DILL
Use another fresh herb such as parsley.

Edamame Avocado Toast

2 SERVINGS 10 MINUTES

INGREDIENTS

1/2 cup Frozen Edamame

1 Avocado (medium, mashed)

3 1/2 ozs Sourdough Bread (toasted)

1/2 oz Pickled Red Onions

1 tsp Sesame Seeds (black)

NUTRITION

AMOUNT PER SERVING

Calories	343	Carbs	37g
Fat	18g	Protein	12g

DIRECTIONS

01 Cook the edamame in salted boiling water for three to four minutes. Set aside.

02 Spread the avocado on the toast and top with the edamame, red onions, and sesame seeds. Enjoy!

NOTES

LEFTOVERS
Do not open and mash the avocado until ready to serve. Refrigerate the cooked edamame in an airtight container for up to three days.

SERVING SIZE
One serving is one piece of toast.

ADDITIONAL TOPPINGS
Sprinkle with chilli flakes.

GLUTEN-FREE
Use gluten-free bread.

MORE FLAVOR
Top with olive oil or flavor-infused oil.

Turkey, Avocado & Sun Dried Tomato Sandwich

2 SERVINGS 10 MINUTES

INGREDIENTS

2 tbsps Sun Dried Tomato Pesto

7 1/16 ozs Sourdough Bread (toasted)

1 Avocado (medium, sliced)

6 1/16 ozs Sliced Turkey Breast

1 cup Arugula

NUTRITION

AMOUNT PER SERVING

Calories	545	**Carbs**	61g
Fat	20g	**Protein**	26g

DIRECTIONS

01 Spread the pesto onto the toast. Top with avocado, sliced turkey, and arugula. Close the sandwich and enjoy!

NOTES

LEFTOVERS
Best enjoyed immediately or refrigerate in an airtight container for up to two days.

SERVING SIZE
One serving is equal to one sandwich.

MORE FLAVOR
Add tomato and red onion.

GLUTEN-FREE
Use gluten-free bread instead.

SOURDOUGH BREAD
One slice of sourdough bread is equal to approximately 1 3/4 oz or 50 grams.

Edamame Ricotta Toast

2 SERVINGS 10 MINUTES

INGREDIENTS

1/4 cup Ricotta Cheese

1 tsp Lemon Juice

3/4 cup Frozen Edamame (thawed, divided)

Sea Salt & Black Pepper (to taste)

3 1/2 ozs Sourdough Bread (toasted)

NUTRITION

AMOUNT PER SERVING

Calories	241	Carbs	31g
Fat	6g	Protein	14g

DIRECTIONS

01 Add ricotta, lemon juice, and 2/3 of the edamame to the bowl of a food processor. Process until smooth. Season with salt and pepper.

02 Spread the ricotta mixture onto the toast. Top with the remaining edamame. Enjoy!

NOTES

LEFTOVERS
Refrigerate the edamame ricotta mixture in an airtight container for up to three days. Spread onto bread when ready to serve.

SERVING SIZE
One serving is equal to one piece of toast.

MORE FLAVOR
Add tomato and cucumber.

ADDITIONAL TOPPINGS
Add fresh herbs such as dill or parsley.

GLUTEN-FREE
Use gluten-free bread instead.

SOURDOUGH BREAD
One slice of sourdough bread is equal to approximately 1 3/4 oz or 50 grams.

Edamame Cream Cheese Toast

1 SERVING 10 MINUTES

INGREDIENTS

1/2 cup Frozen Edamame

3 1/2 ozs Sourdough Bread (toasted)

3 tbsps Cream Cheese, Regular

1/4 cup Broccoli Sprouts

Sea Salt & Black Pepper (to taste)

NUTRITION

AMOUNT PER SERVING

Calories	480	**Carbs**	57g
Fat	17g	**Protein**	22g

DIRECTIONS

01   Cook the edamame in salted boiling water for three to four minutes.

02   Top the sourdough toast with cream cheese, edamame, broccoli sprouts, salt, and pepper. Enjoy!

NOTES

LEFTOVERS
Refrigerate leftovers in an airtight container and consume within one day for best results.

SERVING SIZE
One serving is two pieces of toast.

MAKE IT VEGAN
Omit the cream cheese. Use vegan cream cheese, mashed avocado, or hummus instead.

ADDITIONAL TOPPINGS
Sprinkle with chilli flakes.

GLUTEN-FREE
Use gluten-free bread instead.

MORE FLAVOR
Top with extra virgin olive oil or flavor-infused oil.

SOURDOUGH BREAD
One slice of sourdough bread is equal to approximately 1 3/4 oz or 50 grams.

Smashed Edamame & Mushroom Sandwich

1 SERVING 20 MINUTES

INGREDIENTS

1 1/2 tsps Extra Virgin Olive Oil (divided)

2/3 cup Mushrooms (sliced)

Sea Salt & Black Pepper (to taste)

1/2 cup Frozen Edamame (thawed)

1 tsp Lemon Juice

1/3 cup Arugula

3 1/2 ozs Sourdough Bread (toasted)

NUTRITION

AMOUNT PER SERVING

Calories	418	**Carbs**	57g
Fat	11g	**Protein**	21g

DIRECTIONS

01 In a pan over medium-high heat, add half of the oil and mushrooms. Sauté until golden brown and season with salt and pepper.

02 In a bowl, add the edamame, lemon juice, and the remaining oil. Lightly smash with a fork and season with salt and pepper.

03 Spread the smashed edamame on the toasted bread. Top with mushrooms and arugula. Close the sandwich and enjoy!

NOTES

LEFTOVERS
Refrigerate in an airtight container for up to three days.

SERVING SIZE
One serving is equal to one sandwich.

MORE FLAVOR
Add chili flakes and onion powder.

ADDITIONAL TOPPINGS
Add cucumber and tomato.

GLUTEN-FREE
Use gluten-free bread instead of sourdough.

SOURDOUGH BREAD
One slice of sourdough bread is equal to approximately 1 3/4 oz or 50 grams.

Panzanella with Prosciutto

2 SERVINGS 20 MINUTES

INGREDIENTS

1 tbsp Extra Virgin Olive Oil

1/2 tsp Lemon Juice

1 tsp Italian Seasoning

1 cup Cherry Tomatoes (halved)

1 Cucumber (medium, thinly sliced)

3 1/2 ozs Sourdough Bread (cubed, toasted)

2 ozs Mozzarella Ball (thorn into pieces)

Sea Salt & Black Pepper (to taste)

2 tbsps Basil Leaves

2 ozs Prosciutto

NUTRITION

AMOUNT PER SERVING

Calories	366	**Carbs**	33g
Fat	17g	**Protein**	20g

DIRECTIONS

01   Add the oil, lemon juice, and Italian seasoning to a large bowl. Add the tomatoes, cucumber, toasted bread, and mozzarella and toss to combine. Season with salt and pepper.

02   Top with basil and proscuitto. Divide evenly between plates and enjoy!

NOTES

LEFTOVERS
Refrigerate in an airtight container for up to two days.

SERVING SIZE
One serving is equal to approximately 1 1/2 cups.

GLUTEN-FREE
Use gluten-free bread instead.

MORE FLAVOR
Add soft boiled egg.

ADDITIONAL TOPPINGS
Chopped parsley or fresh dill.

MAKE IT VEGAN
Omit the prosciutto. Top with chickpeas.

Cucumber & Hummus Open Face Sandwich

1 SERVING 5 MINUTES

INGREDIENTS

1 3/4 ozs Sourdough Bread

2 tsps Hummus

1/4 Cucumber (medium, sliced)

1 stalk Green Onion (thinly sliced)

2 tbsps Fresh Dill (chopped)

Sea Salt & Black Pepper (to taste)

NUTRITION

AMOUNT PER SERVING

Calories	163	**Carbs**	29g
Fat	2g	**Protein**	6g

DIRECTIONS

01 Cut each slice of bread in half and top with hummus, cucumber, green onion, dill, salt, and pepper. Enjoy!

NOTES

LEFTOVERS
Best enjoyed immediately.
GLUTEN-FREE
Use gluten-free bread.
ADDITIONAL TOPPINGS
Lemon juice, hot sauce, chili flakes, and/or fresh parsley.
SOURDOUGH BREAD
One slice of sourdough bread is equal to approximately 1 3/4 oz or 50 grams.

Turmeric Chickpea Sandwich

3 SERVINGS 10 MINUTES

INGREDIENTS

11 2/3 ozs Chickpeas (cooked)

3 ozs Vegan Mayonnaise

1/2 tsp Turmeric

Sea Salt & Black Pepper (to taste)

6 slices Sourdough Bread

1 2/3 ozs Baby Spinach

1 Tomato (medium, sliced)

NUTRITION

AMOUNT PER SERVING

Calories	484	Carbs	56g
Fat	24g	Protein	13g

DIRECTIONS

01 Use the back of a fork to smash the chickpeas. Stir in the mayonnaise, turmeric, salt and pepper until well combined.

02 Scoop the turmeric chickpea mixture onto the bread. Add the spinach and tomato. Close the sandwich and enjoy!

NOTES

LEFTOVERS
Refrigerate in an airtight container for up to one day.

GLUTEN-FREE
Use gluten-free bread instead.

MORE FLAVOR
Add onion powder and minced garlic. Toast the bread.

ADDITIONAL TOPPINGS
Add cucumber, sliced green onions, diced celery, or red onion.

SAVE TIME
Blend the chickpeas, mayonnaise, turmeric, salt and pepper in a food processor to your desired consistency.

Roasted Vegetable Sandwich

2 SERVINGS 20 MINUTES

INGREDIENTS

1 Zucchini (sliced length-wise)

1 Eggplant (Chinese, sliced length-wise)

Sea Salt & Black Pepper (to taste)

3 tbsps Green Goddess Salad Dressing

7 1/16 ozs Sourdough Bread (toasted)

1 cup Baby Spinach

4 ozs Roasted Red Peppers

NUTRITION

AMOUNT PER SERVING

Calories	445	**Carbs**	71g
Fat	11g	**Protein**	14g

DIRECTIONS

01   Preheat the oven to 400°F (205°C) and line a baking sheet with parchment paper.

02   Arrange the sliced zucchini and eggplant onto the baking sheet and sprinkle with salt and pepper. Bake for 12 to 15 minutes or until soft and cooked through.

03   Spread the dressing on the toasted bread. Top with spinach, zucchini, eggplant, and roasted red peppers. Close the sandwich and enjoy!

NOTES

LEFTOVERS
Best enjoyed immediately or refrigerate in an airtight container for up to two days.

SERVING SIZE
One serving is equal to one sandwich.

GLUTEN-FREE
Use gluten-free bread instead of sourdough.

MORE FLAVOR
Season the eggplant and zucchini with paprika, chili flakes and/or garlic powder.

ADDITIONAL TOPPINGS
Add cucumber, tomato, and/or chickpeas.

NO GREEN GODDESS DRESSING
Use hummus, pesto, or any other dressing.

SOURDOUGH BREAD
One slice of sourdough bread is equal to approximately 1 3/4 oz or 50 grams.

Whipped Ricotta & Avocado Toast

1 SERVING 10 MINUTES

INGREDIENTS

1/4 cup Ricotta Cheese

1/2 Lemon (juice and zested)

1 3/4 ozs Sourdough Bread (toasted)

1/2 Avocado (sliced)

1/2 tsp Mint Leaves (chopped)

Sea Salt & Black Pepper (to taste)

NUTRITION

AMOUNT PER SERVING

Calories	383	Carbs	39g
Fat	21g	Protein	12g

DIRECTIONS

01 In a food processor, whip together the ricotta cheese, lemon juice, and zest until smooth.

02 Spread the whipped ricotta over the toasted bread. Slice the avocado and place it on top. Sprinkle with chopped mint, sea salt, and black pepper. Enjoy!

NOTES

LEFTOVERS
Refrigerate the whipped ricotta in an airtight container for up to four days.

GLUTEN-FREE
Use gluten free bread.

DAIRY-FREE
Use soft vegan cheese instead of ricotta.

ADDITIONAL TOPPINGS
Cherry tomatoes, chili flakes, and/or jalapeno.

SOURDOUGH BREAD
One slice of sourdough bread is equal to approximately 1 3/4 oz or 50 grams.

Chicken Salad Sandwich

2 SERVINGS 10 MINUTES

INGREDIENTS

5 ozs Chicken Breast, Cooked (shredded)

2 stalks Celery (chopped)

1/4 cup Red Onion (finely chopped)

2 tbsps Parsley (finely chopped)

1/4 cup Plain Greek Yogurt

1/4 Lemon (juced, zested)

Sea Salt & Black Pepper (to taste)

7 ozs Sourdough Bread (toasted)

NUTRITION

AMOUNT PER SERVING

Calories	394	Carbs	53g
Fat	3g	Protein	35g

DIRECTIONS

01 In a medium-sized bowl, add the chicken, celery, onion, parsley, Greek yogurt, lemon juice, zest, salt, and pepper. Mix well to incorporate.

02 Spread the chicken evenly over one slice of sourdough. Close the sandwich and enjoy!

NOTES

LEFTOVERS
Refrigerate the chicken in an airtight container for up to two days.

SERVING SIZE
One serving is one sandwich.

GLUTEN-FREE
Use gluten-free bread instead.

DAIRY-FREE
Use dairy-free unsweetened yogurt or replace the yogurt with mayonnaise.

SOURDOUGH BREAD
One slice of sourdough bread is equal to approximately 1 3/4 oz or 50 grams.

White Bean Purée & Sautéed Mushrooms on Toast

2 SERVINGS 20 MINUTES

INGREDIENTS

1 1/2 cups White Navy Beans (cooked, rinsed)

1 tsp Lemon Juice

2 tbsps Extra Virgin Olive Oil (divided)

Sea Salt & Black Pepper (to taste)

8 White Button Mushrooms (sliced)

3 1/2 ozs Sourdough Bread (toasted)

1 tbsp Parsley (chopped)

NUTRITION

AMOUNT PER SERVING

Calories	453	**Carbs**	62g
Fat	15g	**Protein**	18g

DIRECTIONS

01 In a food processor, purée the white beans, lemon juice, and half of the olive oil until smooth. Season with salt and pepper to taste.

02 In a medium pan over high heat, add the remaining olive oil. Once the oil is hot, sauté the sliced mushrooms for two to three minutes or until cooked and golden brown. Season with salt and pepper to taste.

03 Spread the white bean purée evenly on top of the toasted bread.

04 Top with sautéed mushrooms and chopped parsley. Enjoy.

NOTES

LEFTOVERS
Refrigerate the white bean purée and sautéed mushrooms in separate airtight containers for up to three days.

SERVING SIZE
One serving is equal to approximately 2/3 cup white bean purée and 1/8 cup sautéed mushrooms on one slice of sourdough bread.

MORE FLAVOR
Add garlic to the purée and thyme to the sautéed mushrooms.

ADDITIONAL TOPPINGS
Chili flakes and/or fresh mint.

SOURDOUGH BREAD
One slice of sourdough bread is equal to approximately 1 3/4 oz or 50 grams.

Smashed Chickpea Toast

1 SERVING 15 MINUTES

INGREDIENTS

1 cup Chickpeas (cooked, rinsed)

1 tsp Extra Virgin Olive Oil

2 tbsps Lemon Juice

1 Garlic (clove, minced)

1/4 tsp Sea Salt

1/4 tsp Black Pepper

1/4 tsp Oregano

1 tsp Fresh Dill (chopped)

1 3/4 ozs Sourdough Bread (toasted)

NUTRITION

AMOUNT PER SERVING

Calories	447	**Carbs**	73g
Fat	9g	**Protein**	20g

DIRECTIONS

01 In a small bowl, add the chickpeas, olive oil, lemon juice, garlic, salt, pepper and oregano. Lightly smash with a fork.

02 Add the dill and mix. Taste and add more flavor if desired.

03 Pour the smashed chickpeas onto the toasted bread and spread it out with a fork.

04 Cut the toast in half and enjoy!

NOTES

LEFTOVERS
Best enjoyed right away.

SOURDOUGH BREAD
One slice of sourdough bread is equal to approximately 1 3/4 oz or 50 grams.

GLUTEN-FREE
Use gluten-free bread.

MORE FLAVOR
Rub garlic onto the toast before adding the smashed chickpeas.

ADDITIONAL TOPPINGS
Top with hemp seeds, dill, green onions, basil, chili flakes.

Avocado Toast with Tofu Scramble

1 SERVING 15 MINUTES

INGREDIENTS

6 ozs Silken Tofu (drained)

1 1/2 tsps Nutritional Yeast

1/2 tsp Garlic Powder

1/4 tsp Paprika

1/8 tsp Sea Salt

1 3/4 ozs Sourdough Bread (toasted)

1/2 Avocado (sliced)

NUTRITION

AMOUNT PER SERVING

Calories	402	Carbs	40g
Fat	19g	Protein	18g

DIRECTIONS

01 In a pan over medium heat, add the tofu, nutritional yeast, garlic powder, paprika, and salt. Use the spatula to stir and gently break up the tofu. Cook until the edges are firm and liquid is gone, about 15 minutes.

02 Top the sourdough with avocado and the scrambled tofu. Add more salt if desired. Enjoy!

NOTES

LEFTOVERS
Refrigerate in an airtight container for up to three days.

MORE FLAVOR
Add black pepper, turmeric, and black salt.

ADDITIONAL TOPPINGS
Serve it with salsa or fresh fruit.

SOURDOUGH BREAD
One slice of sourdough bread is equal to approximately 1 3/4 oz or 50 grams.

Green Goddess Sandwich

2 SERVINGS 15 MINUTES

INGREDIENTS

2 tbsps Water

1 Avocado (medium)

1/2 cup Parsley (stems removed)

1 stalk Green Onion (trimmed)

1/8 tsp Sea Salt

7 ozs Sourdough Bread (toasted)

1/2 cup Microgreens

2 cups Baby Spinach

NUTRITION

AMOUNT PER SERVING

Calories	430	**Carbs**	60g
Fat	15g	**Protein**	13g

DIRECTIONS

01 Add the water, avocado, parsley, green onion, and salt to a food processor. Blend until smooth.

02 Spread the sauce evenly over each slice of sourdough. Add the microgreens and spinach. Close the sandwich and enjoy!

NOTES

LEFTOVERS
Best enjoyed immediately or refrigerate in an airtight container for up to two days.

SERVING SIZE
One serving is one sandwich.

GLUTEN-FREE
Use gluten-free bread instead of sourdough.

MORE FLAVOR
Add red pepper flakes, garlic, or lime juice.

ADDITIONAL TOPPINGS
Add cucumber slices, red onion, tomato, chickpeas, or cheese.

NO SPINACH
Use arugula, mixed greens, or kale instead.

SOURDOUGH BREAD
One slice of sourdough bread is equal to approximately 1 3/4 oz or 50 grams.

Omelette with Toast & Banana

1 SERVING 10 MINUTES

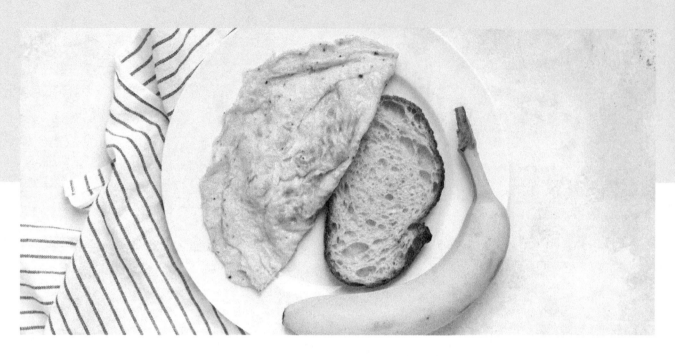

INGREDIENTS

3 Egg
Sea Salt & Black Pepper (to taste)
1 tsp Extra Virgin Olive Oil
1 3/4 ozs Sourdough Bread (toasted)
1 Banana

NUTRITION

AMOUNT PER SERVING

Calories	483	**Carbs**	52g
Fat	19g	**Protein**	25g

DIRECTIONS

01 Whisk the eggs in a small bowl and season with salt and pepper to taste.

02 Heat the oil in a pan over medium heat. Add the eggs and cook until almost set. Fold in half and transfer the omelette to a plate.

03 Serve with the toast and banana. Enjoy!

NOTES

LEFTOVERS
Best enjoyed immediately but can be refrigerated in an airtight container for up to three days.

GLUTEN-FREE
Use gluten-free bread.

MORE FLAVOR
Add butter or mayonnaise to the toast.

SOURDOUGH BREAD
One slice of sourdough bread is equal to approximately 1 3/4 oz or 50 grams.

Broccoli & Cheese Melt

1 SERVING 15 MINUTES

INGREDIENTS

1/2 cup Broccoli (chopped into florets)

1 1/2 tsps Butter

3 1/2 ozs Sourdough Bread

1 1/2 ozs Cheddar Cheese (shredded)

NUTRITION

AMOUNT PER SERVING

Calories	483	**Carbs**	52g
Fat	20g	**Protein**	20g

DIRECTIONS

01 Steam the broccoli over a small pot of water for about five minutes or until fork tender. Drain and set aside.

02 Heat a skillet over medium-low heat. Spread the butter on the outside of both slices of bread. Add the cheddar and broccoli to the middle.

03 Place on the skillet and cook for about four minutes per side, until browned on both sides. Remove from the skillet and slice in half. Enjoy!

NOTES

LEFTOVERS
Best enjoyed immediately but can be refrigerated in an airtight container for up to two days.

GLUTEN-FREE
Use gluten-free bread.

DAIRY-FREE
Use vegan cheese and vegan mayonnaise.

ADDITIONAL TOPPINGS
Add apple slices, pear slices, or slices of cooked chicken.

SOURDOUGH BREAD
One slice of sourdough bread is equal to approximately 1 3/4 oz or 50 grams.

Slow Cooker French Onion Soup

5 SERVINGS 16 HOURS

INGREDIENTS

3 tbsps Butter

2 tbsps Extra Virgin Olive Oil

6 Yellow Onion (sliced thin)

1/3 oz Thyme Sprigs

3 Bay Leaf

1 1/2 tsps Cane Sugar

5 cups Beef Broth

3/4 cup White Cooking Wine

8 ozs Sourdough Bread

1 1/2 cups Gruyere Cheese (shredded)

NUTRITION

AMOUNT PER SERVING

Calories	454	**Carbs**	38g
Fat	23g	**Protein**	18g

DIRECTIONS

01 Combine the butter, oil, onions, thyme, bay leaves, and sugar into the slow cooker. Cook over low heat for 10 hours.

02 Remove the thyme and bay leaves and discard. Add the beef broth and wine and cook over low heat for six hours. Taste and season with additional salt if necessary.

03 Turn on the broiler. Portion soup into oven-safe bowls and place sourdough on top. Top with cheese and place in the oven to broil for one to two minutes, until golden brown.

04 Remove bowls from the oven and enjoy!

NOTES

LEFTOVERS

Leftover soup can be refrigerated for up to five days, or freeze for longer.

SERVING SIZE

One serving is equal to one 15 ounce bowl.

GLUTEN-FREE

Use a gluten-free bread.

DAIRY-FREE

Use a dairy-free cheese.

NO CANE SUGAR

Use brown sugar or coconut sugar instead.

Seitan Sauerkraut Sandwich

1 SERVING 10 MINUTES

INGREDIENTS

2 tsps Avocado Oil (divided)

2 ozs Seitan (chopped)

2 Cremini Mushrooms (sliced)

1 tbsp Dijon Mustard

3 1/2 ozs Sourdough Bread (toasted)

1/3 cup Sauerkraut (drained)

NUTRITION

AMOUNT PER SERVING

Calories	445	Carbs	58g
Fat	11g	Protein	22g

DIRECTIONS

01   Heat the oil in a pan over medium-high heat. Cook the seitan and mushrooms until soft, about five to eight minutes.

02   Spread the mustard evenly over the toasted sourdough. Top with the mushrooms, seitan, and sauerkraut. Close the sandwich and enjoy!

NOTES

LEFTOVERS
Enjoy immediately for best results or refrigerate in an airtight container for up to two days.

GLUTEN-FREE
Use gluten-free bread.

MORE FLAVOR
Add horseradish and sautéed onions.

SOURDOUGH BREAD
One slice of sourdough bread is equal to approximately 1 3/4 oz or 50 grams.

Melty Cheese & Egg Toast

1 SERVING 10 MINUTES

INGREDIENTS

1 tbsp Extra Virgin Olive Oil (divided)
1 3/4 ozs Sourdough Bread
1 1/3 ozs Cheddar Cheese
1 Egg
Sea Salt & Black Pepper (to taste)

NUTRITION

AMOUNT PER SERVING

Calories	477	**Carbs**	26g
Fat	32g	**Protein**	20g

DIRECTIONS

01 Heat a small skillet over medium heat. Once hot, add 3/4 of the oil and then add the bread. Fry the bread on both sides until lightly browned and crispy.

02 Turn the oven to broil. Place the bread on a baking sheet and top with cheese. Broil until just melted and slightly browned, about one to two minutes.

03 Meanwhile, in the same skillet, add the remaining oil. Cook the egg until the whites are set and the yolk is cooked to your liking. Season with salt and pepper. Serve with the cheesy toast and enjoy!

NOTES

LEFTOVERS
This is best enjoyed immediately after making.
GLUTEN-FREE
Use gluten-free bread instead.
DAIRY-FREE
Use dairy-free cheese instead.
SOURDOUGH BREAD
One slice of sourdough bread is equal to approximately 1 3/4 oz or 50 grams.

Tomato & Chive Open Face Sandwich

1 SERVING 10 MINUTES

INGREDIENTS

2 tbsps Cream Cheese, Regular

1 3/4 ozs Sourdough Bread

1/2 Tomato (sliced)

1/4 tsp Everything Bagel Seasoning

1 tsp Chives (chopped)

NUTRITION

AMOUNT PER SERVING

Calories	223	Carbs	27g
Fat	9g	Protein	8g

DIRECTIONS

01 Spread the cream cheese on the sourdough. Top with the tomato slices. Add the everything bagel seasoning and chives on top. Enjoy!

NOTES

LEFTOVERS
Best enjoyed when made fresh.

GLUTEN-FREE
Use gluten-free bread or tortilla instead.

DAIRY-FREE
Use a dairy-free cream cheese.

ADDITIONAL TOPPINGS
Basil, green onions, balsamic vinegar, salt, and pepper.

SOURDOUGH BREAD
One slice of sourdough bread is equal to approximately 1 3/4 oz or 50 grams.

Fried Egg BLT

1 SERVING 5 MINUTES

INGREDIENTS

1 tsp Extra Virgin Olive Oil

1 Egg

Sea Salt & Black Pepper (to taste)

1 tsp Mayonnaise

3 1/2 ozs Sourdough Bread (toasted)

1/16 head Green Lettuce (leaves separated)

1/2 Tomato (sliced)

2 slices Bacon, Cooked

NUTRITION

AMOUNT PER SERVING

Calories	490	Carbs	50g
Fat	20g	Protein	22g

DIRECTIONS

01 In a small pan, heat the oil over medium heat.

02 Cook the egg in the pan until the whites are set and the yolk is cooked to your liking. Season with salt and pepper. Remove and set aside.

03 Spread the mayonnaise over the toasted bread. Add the toppings, leaving the egg until last. Slice in half and enjoy!

NOTES

LEFTOVERS
Best enjoyed freshly made.

GLUTEN-FREE
Use gluten-free bread instead.

ADDITIONAL TOPPINGS
Avocado, red pepper flakes, fresh herbs.

SOURDOUGH BREAD
One slice of sourdough bread is equal to approximately 1 3/4 oz or 50 grams.

Smoked Salmon Open-Face Sandwich

1 SERVING 5 MINUTES

INGREDIENTS

1 3/4 ozs Sourdough Bread

1 1/2 tbsps Cream Cheese, Regular

1/8 Cucumber (thinly sliced)

Sea Salt & Black Pepper (to taste)

2 ozs Smoked Salmon

1 tbsp Red Onion (thinly sliced)

2 tbsps Sunflower Sprouts (optional)

NUTRITION

AMOUNT PER SERVING

Calories	272	**Carbs**	27g
Fat	9g	**Protein**	17g

DIRECTIONS

01 Spread the cream cheese on the sourdough. Top with the cucumber slices and season with salt and pepper. Add the smoked salmon, onion, and sprouts on top. Enjoy!

NOTES

LEFTOVERS
This is best enjoyed immediately after making.

GLUTEN-FREE
Use gluten-free bread or a tortilla instead.

DAIRY-FREE
Use a dairy-free cream cheese.

ADDITIONAL TOPPINGS
Capers and/or fresh herbs.

SOURDOUGH BREAD
One slice of sourdough bread is equal to approximately 1 3/4 oz or 50 grams.

Tuna Avocado Sandwich

1 SERVING 10 MINUTES

INGREDIENTS

1 can Tuna

Sea Salt & Black Pepper (to taste)

1 stalk Celery (finely chopped)

2 tbsps Red Onion (finely chopped)

1/2 Avocado (medium)

3 1/2 ozs Sourdough Bread (toasted)

NUTRITION

AMOUNT PER SERVING

Calories	566	**Carbs**	60g
Fat	16g	**Protein**	44g

DIRECTIONS

01 In a small bowl add the tuna, salt and pepper, celery, and red onion. Mix together until well combined. Add the avocado and mash into the tuna mixture.

02 Scoop the tuna on top of one of the slices of bread and place the other slice on top. Slice and enjoy!

NOTES

LEFTOVERS
Refrigerate the tuna in an airtight container for up to three days. For best results, mix with the avocado and serve it on the bread just before enjoying.

GLUTEN-FREE
Use gluten-free bread instead.

CANNED TUNA
One can of tuna is equal to 165 grams or 5.8 ounces, drained.

NO RED ONION
Use chives or green onions instead.

NO AVOCADO
Use mayonnaise or Greek yogurt instead.

SOURDOUGH BREAD
One slice of sourdough bread is equal to approximately 1 3/4 oz or 50 grams.

Classic Grilled Cheese Sandwich

1 SERVING 10 MINUTES

INGREDIENTS

1 1/2 tsps Butter

3 1/2 ozs Sourdough Bread

1 1/16 ozs Cheddar Cheese (grated)

NUTRITION

AMOUNT PER SERVING

Calories	422	**Carbs**	49g
Fat	16g	**Protein**	17g

DIRECTIONS

01 Heat a skillet over medium-low heat.

02 Spread the butter on the outside of both slices of bread. Add the cheddar to the middle.

03 Place on the skillet and cook for about four minutes per side, until browned on both sides. Remove from the skillet, slice in half. Enjoy!

NOTES

LEFTOVERS
This is best enjoyed immediately after making.

GLUTEN-FREE
Use gluten-free bread instead.

DAIRY-FREE
Use a dairy-free cheddar style cheese.

NO BUTTER
Spread mayonnaise on each outside slice of bread instead.

MAKE IT VEGAN
Use a vegan butter and vegan cheese.

SOURDOUGH BREAD
One slice of sourdough bread is equal to approximately 1 3/4 oz or 50 grams.

Egg Salad Sandwich

2 SERVINGS 15 MINUTES

INGREDIENTS

4 Egg
2 tbsps Mayonnaise
1/8 tsp Turmeric (ground)
Sea Salt & Black Pepper (to taste)
7 ozs Sourdough Bread (toasted)
3 tbsps Sunflower Sprouts (optional)

NUTRITION

AMOUNT PER SERVING

Calories	489	**Carbs**	49g
Fat	20g	**Protein**	22g

DIRECTIONS

01 In a medium-sized pot add the eggs and cover with water. Bring to a boil, and then turn off the heat and remove from heat. Cover and let stand for 10 minutes.

02 Remove the eggs and let cool, then peel and add to a bowl. Add the mayonnaise, turmeric, salt, and pepper. Mash with a fork to desired consistency.

03 Add egg salad to a slice of sourdough and top with sprouts and then the other slice of sourdough. Slice and enjoy!

NOTES

LEFTOVERS
Refrigerate the egg salad for up to three days. Toast the bread fresh for best results.

GLUTEN-FREE
Use a gluten free bread.

MORE FLAVOR
Add a pinch of cayenne.

ADDITIONAL TOPPINGS
Add chives or chopped red onion.

NO SPROUTS
Omit or replace with lettuce.

SOURDOUGH BREAD
One slice of sourdough bread is equal to approximately 1 3/4 oz or 50 grams.

Turkey Hummus Sandwich

1 SERVING 5 MINUTES

INGREDIENTS

2 slices Bread

4 ozs Turkey Breast, Cooked

1 tbsp Hummus

1 1/2 tsps Dijon Mustard

1/2 cup Mixed Greens

NUTRITION

AMOUNT PER SERVING

Calories	356	**Carbs**	27g
Fat	10g	**Protein**	39g

DIRECTIONS

01   Lightly toast the bread.

02   Spread one slice of the bread with hummus and mustard. Layer on the turkey and mixed greens. Place the second slice of bread over top. Slice and enjoy!

NOTES

NO TURKEY
Use chicken breast instead.

VEGAN & VEGETARIAN
Use smashed chickpeas instead of turkey.

GLUTEN-FREE
Use gluten-free bread instead or make it as a lettuce wrap.

Toast with Almond Butter & Peaches

1 SERVING 5 MINUTES

INGREDIENTS

2 1/2 tbsps Almond Butter

3 1/2 ozs Sourdough Bread (toasted)

1 Peach (sliced)

1/8 tsp Cinnamon

NUTRITION

AMOUNT PER SERVING

Calories	547	Carbs	70g
Fat	22g	Protein	19g

DIRECTIONS

01 Spread the almond butter onto the toast. Top with the peach slices and cinnamon. Enjoy!

NOTES

LEFTOVERS
Best enjoyed fresh.

GLUTEN-FREE
Use gluten-free bread instead.

NUT-FREE
Use sunflower seed butter instead of almond butter.

LIKES IT SWEET
Add honey.

SOURDOUGH BREAD
One slice of sourdough bread is equal to approximately 1 3/4 oz or 50 grams.

Almond Butter & Banana Sandwich

1 SERVING 5 MINUTES

INGREDIENTS

2 tbsps Almond Butter

3 1/2 ozs Sourdough Bread

1/2 Banana (sliced into rounds)

NUTRITION

AMOUNT PER SERVING

Calories	492	**Carbs**	67g
Fat	18g	**Protein**	17g

DIRECTIONS

01 Spread the almond butter onto the bread. Top with bananas. Close the sandwich and slice. Enjoy!

NOTES

LEFTOVERS
Refrigerate in an airtight container for up to one day. Best enjoyed fresh.

GLUTEN-FREE
Use gluten free bread.

NUT-FREE
Use sunflower seed butter instead of almond butter.

MORE FLAVOR
Add a dash of cinnamon.

LIKES IT SWEET
Add honey.

SOURDOUGH BREAD
One slice of sourdough bread is equal to approximately 1 3/4 oz or 50 grams.

Fried Egg with Green Onions on Toast

1 SERVING 10 MINUTES

INGREDIENTS

1 1/2 tsps Extra Virgin Olive Oil
1 Egg
1 slice Bread (toasted)
2 stalks Green Onion (sliced)
Sea Salt & Black Pepper (to taste)

NUTRITION

AMOUNT PER SERVING

Calories	215	**Carbs**	14g
Fat	14g	**Protein**	8g

DIRECTIONS

01 Heat olive oil in a frying pan over medium heat. Fry egg and place on top of toast.

02 Turn heat to low-medium and cook green onions until soft, about 1-2 minutes. Season with salt and pepper to taste, and sprinkle on top of the egg. Enjoy!

NOTES

MAKE IT QUICKER
Skip the Green Onion.

Open-Face Tuna Melt

2 SERVINGS 10 MINUTES

INGREDIENTS

1 can Tuna (drained and flaked)

2 stalks Celery (thinly sliced)

1/2 cup Plain Greek Yogurt

1 1/2 tsps Apple Cider Vinegar

1 tbsp Dijon Mustard

1 1/2 tsps Fresh Dill

1 tsp Garlic Powder

1 1/3 ozs Swiss Cheese (sliced or shredded)

2 slices Bread

NUTRITION

AMOUNT PER SERVING

Calories	291	**Carbs**	18g
Fat	11g	**Protein**	29g

DIRECTIONS

01 Adjust oven rack to the top, closest to the broiler. Set oven to low broil.

02 In a bowl, combine tuna, celery, yogurt, apple cider vinegar, dijon, dill and garlic powder.

03 Scoop tuna mixture onto bread and spread evenly. Top with Swiss cheese.

04 Broil in oven for about 3 to 5 minutes, or until cheese is melted and slightly browned. Watch closely for burning and do not leave unattended.

05 Remove from oven and enjoy!

NOTES

LOADED TUNA MELT
Add minced red onion, sliced tomato and avocado.

CANNED TUNA
One can of tuna is equal to 165 grams or 5.8 ounces, drained.

VEGAN AND VEGETARIAN
Use mashed chickpeas instead of tuna, avocado instead of yogurt and omit the cheese.

GLUTEN-FREE
Use gluten-free bread or serve on a brown rice tortilla.

Soft Scrambled Eggs on Toast

2 SERVINGS 5 MINUTES

INGREDIENTS

4 Egg
1/2 tsp Butter
3 1/2 ozs Sourdough Bread (toasted)
1 tbsp Chives (chopped)
Sea Salt & Black Pepper (to taste)

NUTRITION

AMOUNT PER SERVING

Calories	277	**Carbs**	25g
Fat	10g	**Protein**	17g

DIRECTIONS

01 Crack the eggs into a bowl and whisk well.

02 Heat a skillet over medium-low heat and once hot, add the butter. Once melted, add the eggs to the pan and move them around with a spatula continuously. Keep pushing the eggs around the skillet until fluffy and barely set, about 2 minutes. They should still look slightly runny on top.

03 Divide the eggs onto toast, and top with chives, salt and pepper. Enjoy!

NOTES

LEFTOVERS
For best results, enjoy freshly made.
GLUTEN-FREE
Use gluten-free bread instead.
ADDITIONAL TOPPINGS
Chili flakes and/or fresh herbs like parsley and dill.
NO BUTTER
Use ghee or another cooking oil.
SOURDOUGH BREAD
One slice of sourdough bread is equal to approximately 1 3/4 oz or 50 grams.

Egg Whites with Toast

1 SERVING 5 MINUTES

INGREDIENTS

1 tbsp Avocado Oil

1/2 cup Egg Whites

1/8 tsp Sea Salt

1 3/4 ozs Sourdough Bread (toasted)

NUTRITION

AMOUNT PER SERVING

Calories	311	**Carbs**	25g
Fat	14g	**Protein**	18g

DIRECTIONS

01 Heat the oil in a pan over medium to high heat.

02 Add the egg whites to the skillet and season with salt. Gently stir until cooked through, about 3 to 4 minutes. Adjust salt as needed.

03 Serve the cooked egg whites alongside or on top of the toasted sourdough. Enjoy!

NOTES

LEFTOVERS
Refrigerate in an airtight container for up to four days. Store the egg whites separately and toast the bread just before serving for best results.

GLUTEN-FREE
Use gluten-free bread or sweet potato toast.

ADDITIONAL TOPPINGS
Top with tomato slices, green onion, mushrooms, avocado, bacon, nutritional yeast, cheese, fresh or sautéed greens and/or black pepper.

MAKE IT VEGAN
Use crumbled firm tofu instead of eggs.

SOURDOUGH BREAD
One slice of sourdough bread is equal to approximately 1 3/4 oz or 50 grams.

Egg Whites with Mushrooms & Chives on Toast

1 SERVING 10 MINUTES

INGREDIENTS

1 tbsp Avocado Oil

1/4 cup Oyster Mushrooms (sliced)

1/2 cup Egg Whites

1/8 tsp Sea Salt

1 3/4 ozs Sourdough Bread (toasted)

1 tsp Dried Chives

NUTRITION

AMOUNT PER SERVING

Calories	324	Carbs	27g
Fat	14g	Protein	19g

DIRECTIONS

01 Heat avocado oil in a large skillet over medium heat. Cook the mushrooms until browned, about 3 to 5 minutes. Set aside.

02 Add the egg whites to the skillet and season with salt. Gently stir until cooked through, about 2 to 3 minutes.

03 Transfer the cooked egg whites onto the toasted bread. Top with mushrooms and dried chives. Enjoy!

NOTES

LEFTOVERS

Refrigerate in an airtight container for up to two days. For best results, store the bread separately from the eggs and mushrooms to prevent them from getting soggy.

GLUTEN-FREE

Instead of sourdough bread, use gluten-free bread, tortillas, pitas or use lettuce wraps.

OIL-FREE

Use water or broth instead of oil and add more when food begins sticking to the pan.

MORE FLAVOR

Add fresh chives when cooking the mushrooms instead of dried chives.

MAKE IT VEGAN

Use crumbed firm tofu instead of egg whites.

SOURDOUGH BREAD

One slice of sourdough bread is equal to approximately 1 3/4 oz or 50 grams.

Avocado Egg Salad Sandwich

4 SERVINGS 15 MINUTES

INGREDIENTS

6 Egg

1 Avocado

1 cup Baby Spinach (chopped)

1 tbsp Dijon Mustard

1/4 Lemon (juiced)

Sea Salt & Black Pepper (to taste)

8 slices Bread (toasted)

NUTRITION

AMOUNT PER SERVING

Calories	348	**Carbs**	30g
Fat	19g	**Protein**	14g

DIRECTIONS

01   Place eggs in a pot of cold water, bring to a boil, then simmer for 5-6 minutes. Run under cold water to cool. Peel the eggs and chop roughly.

02   In a bowl, mash and combine the chop boiled eggs, avocado, baby spinach, dijon mustard, lemon juice, salt and pepper.

03   Spread onto toast and enjoy!

NOTES

LESS BREAD
Make it an open-face sandwich.

ADD A KICK
Add red chili flakes or hot sauce.

VEGAN
Use mashed chickpeas or white kidney beans instead of eggs.

Made in the USA
Las Vegas, NV
18 April 2024